Contents

Preface

The journey started with a crushed dream. It was a hot, sticky day in late July, 2005. I was lying in a ditch surrounded by dried mud. Tiny gnats floated above my head and bristle-like grass poked at my skin. The sensation of lying there provided a brief reprieve from the pain shooting through my legs. Try as I might, I could not muster the strength to climb back to the road.

While lying there, blankly staring at the wispy clouds above, I was forced to accept the fact that my dream of running a 50-mile ultra-marathon was going to remain just that—a dream.

Five months earlier, while training for what would be the toughest physical goal I ever attempted, I was foolishly over-confident in my abilities. Why not? I had faced adversity before believing hard work coupled with unwavering determination would make it happen.

But I was wrong. My body simply could not take the beating. I had developed plantar fasciitis resulting in me hobbling out of bed each morning. Every step was met with a searing pain that took hours to extinguish. I had also developed shin splints which made me feel as if my lower legs would snap at any moment. To make matters even worse, I developed what felt like a fractured pelvis and my kneecaps hurt so much I had to walk backwards down stairs.

Through all of that I persevered and trained when I could, sometimes missing days at a time in a feeble attempt to heal my broken body. One day while attempting to keep to my training schedule of running 30 miles, I was at the 12-mile mark when two semis passed one another. In an attempt to avoid them I accidentally stepped on loose gravel at the edge of a steep ditch. Most people would have simply adjusted their weight but in my broken-down state, the best I could muster was to frantically wave my arms. With my barely-functional legs I could not respond fast enough and ended up tumbling down the embankment.

1

Oddly, the fall did not hurt as much as the pain from running. At that moment I realized there was no way I would ever be an ultrarunner. The best I could hope for was suffering through a marathon.

After dragging myself out of that ditch I took a few days off before easing back into training. A month later I ran a marathon. But it wasn't the fifty miler I had dreamed of because the race, while fun, felt more like failure than a victory.

Later that winter I began to research better training methods. I was looking for an answer, *any* answer, in order to finish that same 50-miler the following year. My research led me down many paths from low heart rate training to Gallowalking˙. I researched low mileage *and* high mileage training, advances in shoe technologies, custom orthotics, and various braces and devices runners use to support their various ailments.

One day I stumbled across an obscure article in an academic journal where an author was making a case for barefoot running. The hypothesis was simple: running without shoes strengthens your feet and forces you to run with good form. It was an intriguing idea and ran polar opposite to every bit of information I had researched. For me, the selling point was simple—*I used to run barefoot.*

My first attempts at barefoot running occurred way back in 1992 while preparing for high school wrestling.

At the time I was running with a good friend of mine, Jason Saint Amour. We had the idea of running barefoot on asphalt to "toughen our feet." And, in my first experience with minimalist shoes, we would routinely run in wrestling shoes. At the time our friends thought we were crazy. Who knew at the time we were just a couple of early adopters!

Over the next 13 years, I was a sporadic recreational runner. My goals were to keep fit while attempting to maintain a reasonable weight. All the while my waistline was slowly expanding due to my love of beer, bacon, and gas station hot dogs.

Then in 2004, I met my wife Shelly who introduced me to the concept of regular exercise including several weekly runs totaling 10–15 miles. Though I had always enjoyed running, it wasn't until then that I began taking it seriously. During those runs I always wore shoes. It was early in our relationship and I didn't want to reveal my past interest in barefoot running just yet.

Because I was now a semi-serious runner, I felt I needed formal running shoes. A local big-box sporting goods store advertised a major shoe sale. When I arrived, a teenage salesperson named "Duane" helped me by measuring my feet and giving me a few suggestions. I tried on a few pairs, parading back and forth in front of Shelly and Duane. Two pairs were especially comfortable; the padding in both made it feel as if I were walking on marshmallows. It seemed like a good decision. I had what I thought were comfortable running shoes and was now ready to run in a race.

That next year, in 2005, we decided to run a 15K road race. Even though running in shoes over longer distances felt strange, I adapted the same technique I saw other runners using. They would land on their heel and roll their foot forward. For me it still felt awkward, but seemed to work. Even though that particular race was fun and went well, I did lose several toe nails and did experience pain. Undeterred, the following day I committed to a 50-mile race.

The rest of that summer I obsessively worked toward my ultimate goal of successfully running a 50-miler. Unfortunately my body did not cooperate and injuries started piling up. As a result I started skipping one workout a week and relying on ice baths to ease the pain after every run.

As a quick sidebar—ice baths that involve submerging anything above the thighs should be classified as torture. There are certain parts of our anatomy that were not designed to be submerged in 40° water.

A friend who noticed the pain I was experiencing suggested I go to a local specialty running store for new shoes. Apparently

Duane, from the big box retail store, wasn't the expert I assumed. At the running store the salesperson seemed to be more knowledgeable. He had me dip my feet in water and stand on a piece of paper to measure my arches. Apparently they were "normal."

Then he had me walk on a treadmill (barefoot, mind you). He used a term I was vaguely familiar with: pronation. I was a mild overpronator. He gave me what he described as the perfect pair of shoes. When I explained my experience with Duane we shared a good chuckle about my naivety. Duane clearly did not have the shoe fitting expertise the running store could provide.

I went home and resumed training, confident my new professionally-fitted shoes would eliminate my debilitating injuries. I was wrong. The pain multiplied.

Everything culminated on that fateful day when I plunged into the ditch. It was my low point, both literally and figuratively. I never forgot the feeling of complete and total failure, the stabbing pain of defeat, the emptiness of hopelessness. I felt I wasn't capable of *anything*. I had *limitations*.

The following spring, those feelings became the fuel that lead me to immerse myself in the world of barefoot running. There were few resources at the time. Ken Bob Saxton, Ted McDonald, and Rick Roeber had informative websites. Ken Bob ran a discussion group on Yahoo and there were a handful of academic papers. I drank in all I could. I experimented. I practiced. And I challenged myself.

While I would like to say those early days went well, they did not. Instead they were filled with every "rookie" mistake I could make. But I stuck with it and continued to learn and to refine.

That September I finished the 50-miler. I had accomplished the goal that had eluded me the previous year. Over the next few years, I continued to learn about barefoot running, slowly mastered the craft and started a website to share my experiences. I had no idea that simple, poorly-designed website would lead me to where it has.

In 2009, I was invited to join a barefoot running forum on the *Runners World* website. This led to many discussions with both novice and experienced barefoot runners. I came to the realization that I had a lot of information to share. Being a teacher by trade, I enjoy helping to spread knowledge, and started a series of barefoot running clinics. To supplement the clinics, I started writing brief essays on various topics related to barefoot running.

At some point, people started asking for copies which led to printing them in book form. Those were the humble beginnings to this book.

Starting in the fall of 2009, I began to revise and refine the content of that first book by adding information and honing concepts. This new edition of the book is the culmination of my own experiences, the input of hundreds of barefoot runners, a thorough examination of the current research and applications, along with a touch of my own special brand of teaching (i.e.—bad humor). I have even solicited the ideas of barefoot running skeptics. The resulting learning process includes easy-to-understand practical ideas that are free of the dogma that sometimes accompanies barefoot running discussions.

This book will teach you how to run barefoot in a way that is simple, direct, and easy to understand. I do not make wild claims that barefoot running will turn you into an Olympic-caliber athlete or that barefoot running is free from potential risks. The pages are not filled with needless fluff. Well, there's some fluff—I included my 2009 Hallucination 100-mile race report. It was the first 100-miler I finished and the culmination of my barefoot running efforts which are a testament to the information contained in this book.

I am just an ordinary guy of questionable athletic ability. But if I can finish a 100-mile race, you can also accomplish your running ambitions.

My goal is to teach you in the safest, most efficient way, and hopefully inspire *you* to accomplish extraordinary things.

Acknowledgements

This project would not be possible without the unconditional support of my wife Shelly. Your encouragement and love has changed my life. I will be forever grateful. I would also like to thank my crew at the Hallucination 100-Mile Run: Jason Saint Amour, Mark Robillard, Michael Helton, and Stuart Peterson. You guys helped me reach the loftiest of my goals. I would like to thank Rich Elliott for always being one step ahead of me in the crazy department and Pete Kemme for motivating and educating me about the art and  science of physical conditioning. Dirk Wierenga deserves credit for turning this project into something truly special. I would like to thank Tamara Gerken, Joel Wermiel, Todd Johnston, Richard Knobb, Sharon Bylsma, Shelley Viggiano, Ngoc Bui, and Joe Kurnik for their contributions to this project; it would never have gotten off the ground without you. I would like to thank Tim Looney, Jeremiah Cataldo, and Phil Stapert. Your bits of ultra advice got me to the finish line. I would like to thank Ken Bob Saxton, Rick Roeber, and Ted McDonald. You guys were the pioneers that taught me in the beginning. I would like to thank the contributors to the *Runner's World®* Barefoot Running Forum. You guys have taught and inspired me. Many of the ideas presented in this book are the direct result of our many conversations. Finally, I would like to thank the Flying Spaghetti Monster. His Noodly Appendages guided me throughout the creation of this project.

Disclaimer

The material contained in this book is for informational purposes only. The author and anyone else affiliated with the creation or distribution of this information may not be held liable for damages or injuries of any kind allegedly caused or resulting from the use of this material.

Before beginning this or any type of exercise program, it is recommended that you consult with your physician for authorization and clearance.

Furthermore, if you have any medical condition that affects the tactile sensations or blood flow to your feet or legs (diabetes, neuropathy, etc.), you should not attempt barefoot running.

The information contained herein is not intended to, and never should, substitute for the necessity of seeking the advice of a qualified medical professional. It is my sincere desire to provide information that enhances your running experience and allows you to reach your potential. This will only happen if you stay healthy, injury free, and use common sense.

Why Barefoot Running?

People run barefoot for a variety of reasons. I started running barefoot because of injuries incurred while running a 15K, a trail marathon, and a road marathon in traditional running shoes. As I discussed in the preface, I suffered blackened toenails, plantar fasciitis, chronically sore knees and hips, a reoccurring lower back pain, and shin splints. It was if I had aged 20 years! After doing some research, I decided to try barefoot running once a week. Within a week I fell in love with it and abandoned my running shoes. Other people have different reasons for giving it a try, including:

- Don't enjoy running—looking for something to make it fun
- Strengthen their feet
- Reduce injuries
- Inspired by books such as *Born to Run* by Christopher McDougall
- Reminiscent of childhood
- Don't like the feeling of sweaty, smelly socks and shoes
- Long-time runners looking for a new challenge
- Want to run in a more natural way
- Simplifying their lives
- Rebel against society

Remember—you should be in good health before beginning barefoot running or any physical activity.

Interested in Barefoot Running?
Here are encouraging words from others who have switched.

From Barefoot Rick:

There are several reasons why I began running barefoot, and even more why I continue. When I began in October 2003, I was fascinated by the idea that one could run without shoes. I have always loved going barefoot, so this seemed very logical to me. I read up on barefoot running and discovered that barefoot runners experienced far fewer injuries because of the ball/heel foot strike. Shoe companies have always built the heels up too much on their products—even running shoes. The result is heel-striking which can cause knee and leg problems. Since I started running barefoot in October 2003, I have not experienced an injury to my knees or legs. That was not true when I wore shoes. I experienced a stress fracture in my tibial plateau of my left knee and severe clicking in my right knee. Since running barefoot, I have no re-occurrences of problems associated with former injuries.

Here are a few reasons why I continue to run barefoot:

1. Injury-free due to proper foot strike.

2. It feels great!

3. I no longer have to support the running shoe companies.

4. I always have my running "shoes" with me.

5. Creates new challenges when running marathons (after 13 shod marathons, I was looking for a new challenge).

6. I believe it is the way we were created to run.

Barefoot Rick Roeber
http://barefootrunner.org

When learning to run barefoot—go BARE foot, and listen to your bare soles, don't do more than your soles are ready for. Don't put strains or stresses on your feet that are uncomfortable or painful, either to the soles, or the foot. Don't work too hard.

Running should be easy, it should be comfortable, especially while barefoot. Avoiding movements, pressures, etc., which cause pain, discomfort, or seem like work, will teach people to run gently, smoothly, efficiently, and have fun!

Ken Bob Saxton
http://BarefootKenBob.com
http://TheRunningBarefoot.com

From Barefoot Ted McDonald:

Our ancestors moved over the earth ... and found their way into nearly every nook and cranny of the planet ... with their bare or minimally clad feet. The foot has been the primary vehicle of our success as a species, allowing us to fulfill our desire to explore, discover, achieve and eat. Yet, most people these days have come to see their feet as broken appendages, unfit for the real world, sickly and weak, prone to injury, in need of support and padding, doomed to suffer. Why?

Good question. What did happen? What made our feet sick? Did we devolve? Perhaps it has something to do with the shoes we wear?

Well, arguably, we are the first generation of runners who have worked with the hypothesis that more cushioning and support equals safer running and reduced impact. We have concluded that modern surfaces, hard and unforgiving, require ever-thickening sole padding to help counter the shocks of landing, but is that true?

It is counter-intuitive, but the truth is, and studies back this up, that the more you block out the feeling of impact in your feet, the more impact you are likely to put into your body, at the wrong time in your stride, by moving and landing differently than you would if you actually felt what you were doing.

All those nerves on the bottom of your feet have a purpose after all. Dulling them from sensing seems to be a bad idea ... and the dulling seems to set in motion a series of unfortunate events that ultimately leads to movement patterns unknown to our preeminently capable ancestors ... patterns that seem to lead to inefficient movement and injury.

By taking off your shoes, you give your body a chance to reuse some amazingly useful, built-in systems that help you move in a way that need not be jarring nor pounding regardless of the hardness of the terrain. A way of movement that more effectively captures and re-releases stored energy through elasticity in our bodies: the splaying of our forefoot, the arch in our foot, tendons in the lower legs, calves and quads, and form—all positioned ideally to absorb and recoil the energy of movement, smoothly and efficiently, operating in real-time, on the move, a kind of primordial physical intelligence, a birthright of Homo sapiens. This built in recoil system puts to shame the claims of the marshmallow soft, spring-loaded shoes that capture the imagination of so many.

So, what went wrong?

My hunch is that we got unplugged ... detached ... from our own bodies, from our own feet. That disconnect has led to gait patterns and running styles that are unique to a generation of runners ... we the first cohort in the history of the world to run distance with cushioned, high-heeled shoes. I think it is a case of the cure becoming worse than the ailment, the ailment being hard surfaces and tired bodies, trying to continue moving when the safe form of moving has exhausted itself and the feet and legs would normally protest about continuing ... unless you could give it a little relief, i.e., block pain brought on by less-than-best landing patterns, but once it becomes a habit it ends up being a fundamental change in running form ... and in my opinion, a dying branch of cultural evolutionary experimentation.

Does it have to be this way?

Nope. Learning how to master the fundamental human capacity of running, sans shoes, is a lot easier than you think ... and does not require a purchase. Simply take off your shoes ... and start listening to your feet, listening to your body, moving without internal hard edges, with flow. Focus on incrementally redeveloping your feet and lower legs ... one step at a time, giving them a chance to feel the world and grow from interacting with it, learning from it. And become a student of your own body and of movement, share your experiences, learn and be inspired by others. Crack the nut of joyful movement in your own body, your own unique vehicle. The resources are available unlike at any other time for our generation. Google it.

The paradigm shift away from the over-engineered shoe is connected with other shifts in thinking about our bodies and being human. In your barefeet you are more connected to your body, better balanced, more aware, mindful, present. Those characteristics are good qualities to mimic in your mental life. There is a relationship between the two.

Becoming healthy in mind and body is an incredibly effective way to experience happiness it seems, and all my research into this topic leads me to feel confident that if you follow these insights to their logical conclusion, you too will become a happy, healthy and free thinking individual, comfortable and satisfied with the awesome inheritance your feet and body represent.

Barefoot Ted McDonald
http://barefootted.com

Research Into the Relationship Between Athletic Shoes and Foot Injuries

Barefoot running has experienced resurgence in popularity over the last few years. Part of this resurgence is the result of interesting research about the nature of running injuries. Much of which is based on assumptions by runners in thinking the running shoes they use are designed to prevent injuries.

As researchers explore the relationship between injuries and footwear, some interesting relationships appear. In 1989 Dr. B. Marti published one of the first studies that seemed to link shoe properties with injuries. In his research, Marti tested over 5,000 runners that had finished a race. He found that runners that ran in expensive shoes (costing more than $95) were more than twice as likely to have been injured in the last year than runners that ran in cheaper shoes (costing less than $40). Who would ever think the plastic trainers from Walmart would be better than the latest $200 shoes on display in the window of their local running store?

Around the same time, in 1988, Hamill and Bates published a study that seemed to show that shoes improved as they wore out. Oddly, like a fine wine, they improved with age. This was because as the cushioning and motion-control aspects broke down, the foot was allowed to function more naturally. These two studies seemed to indicate the best shoes are old, worn-out, cheap shoes. It is no coincidence that the rate of running injuries was significantly lower prior to the advent of the modern running shoe (Froncioni, 2006). Imagine, running in thin-soled Converse All-Stars being healthier than today's most technically advanced shoes!

Of particular interest to me is the Hamill and Bates study. This is because most shoe manufacturers recommend replacing shoes every 250–300 miles because the materials degrade with use. Perhaps a case of planned obsolescence? After all, products that are designed to wear out in a certain time require the consumer to buy a new version of the product.

Though some may be suspicious of the idea planned obsolescence, there exists significant research that supports the notion that running shoes can significantly increase the occurrence of injuries.

In 1949 Samuel Shulman, a pioneer in investigating the potential perils of shoes, found a dramatic decrease in foot deformities in children who did not wear shoes as small children. Then in 1972 Steele Stewart reiterated this claim by comparing shod and unshod populations. In addition, Steven Robbins and colleagues, in several studies conducted between 1987 and 1995, conducted a series of experiments to empirically measure various characteristics of running in shoes versus barefoot. Among their many findings is the discovery that wearing shoes decreases a runner's ability to judge impact. As such, shod runners produce far greater impact forces when running. This is believed to be a major factor in the development of running injuries. If you doubt this concept, speak to runners using treadmills at your local gym.

Recently in 2008, Craig, Parker, and Callister conducted a thorough search of the existing literature to find any research supporting the prescribing of shoes with elevated, cushioned heels, and pronation control systems to runners. To their surprise there was no research supporting that claim. Let that sink in for a moment. Craig, Parker, and Callister did not find a single peer-reviewed study that supported the use of modern running shoes. None. Nada.

At the same time, barefoot running has an interesting perception within the medical community. Critics of barefoot running often point out that most podiatrists and other such doctors often recommend highly corrective shoes and orthotics as a means of preventing and treating running injuries. While I do not recommend ignoring the advice of your doctor, it is prudent to exercise some skepticism when dealing with common knowledge rather than solid research. There is a tendency to blindly trust medical professionals without considering the possibility that their opinions may be wrong.

During a recent conversation with orthopedic surgeon and blogger Dr. Joseph Froncioni, he compared the medical community's belief in the medical necessity of shoes to the past belief that baby formula was superior to breast milk.

In an attempt to sell more baby formula, manufacturers aggressively marketed their product. They created a market for their formula by convincing the public that it was a necessity. To further validate their message they handed out samples through hospitals and doctor's offices leading to the perception that formula use was supported by the medical community (Baer, 1982). This resulted in many within the medical community recommending baby formula. The result was a huge increase in formula sales and corresponding sharp decline in breastfeeding.

Subsequent research, conducted in the 1980s, proved the the assumptions about baby formula were not only incorrect but potentially dangerous. Research now shows breast milk is vastly superior to baby formula. The proof is on the label of baby formula, which, by law requires formula manufacturers to make a statement about breast milk being recommended over formula.

How does this relate to running shoes? Through clever marketing, shoe manufacturers have convinced the general public that highly-cushioned, supportive shoes are necessary to allow humans to run. Just like the baby formula claims of the past, the medical community is allowing marketing to influence their opinions.

Does this mean shoe companies are evil entities bent on producing legions of injured runners? Absolutely not. Like all manufacturers, shoe companies produce shoes in order to make a profit while meeting consumer demand. For many years this meant producing shoes that sold well. Because there was high consumer demand for cushioned shoes with built-up heels, this is what they manufactured and sold. Today, due to new research, we are beginning to see a gradual shift in shoe design. As more convincing bio-mechanical research is conducted and consumers begin demanding more minimal shoes, the shoe manufacturers will respond with more offerings.

Note, these current studies supporting barefoot running are of a bio-mechanical nature. Essentially, the studies make an assumption that the improved biomechanics of barefoot running will reduce injuries. While anecdotal evidence seems to support this, until research is conducted comparing shod running to barefoot running, those assumptions should be made with an understanding that actual injury rates have not been measured.

Researchers such as Dr. Daniel Lieberman of Harvard University and Dr. Irene Davis of the University of Delaware are investigating injury rates of barefoot versus shod runners. While this research is ongoing, the current peer-reviewed empirical research supports the adaptation of minimalist shoes and/or barefoot running to help improve form and reduce the incidence of injuries.

The following essay was written by orthopedic surgeon Dr. Joseph Froncioni, and reprinted with his permission. In my opinion, this is the single best summation of the rationale behind the barefoot and minimalist shoe running movement.

This essay can also be found online at:

http://www.quickswood.com/my_weblog/2006/08/athletic_footwe.html

Athletic Footwear and Running Injuries:
Essay on the harmful effects of modern running shoes.

Part 1—Introduction and History

Look, if anyone displayed brand-loyalty, it was me. I LOVED my NIKE AIR MAX Triax™ runners. I wouldn't buy anything else. Why? Because they felt good. I liked the cushioning. I liked the ride. I also felt they protected me from the hard road by interposing a layer of air between the sole of my foot and the pavement. So why was I sidelined with a heel injury for over two months? I listened to the manufacturer and changed my runners every 400 miles. Come to think of it, why do I see so many runners with lower extremity injuries in my office? The traditional answer to these questions has always been overuse often compounded by an underlying mechanical abnormality such as over-pronation or flat-feet.

The treatment, along with modification of training, physiotherapy, stretching etc. has always included a close look at the runner's footwear, often with recommendations about motion control, stability, cushioning, orthotics or custom molded insoles. A growing body of literature in the field of sports medicine, however, is causing a bit of a stir ... no, call it PANIC in the running world. Everything you and I always believed about running shoes and running injuries may be wrong! Here's the scoop: The modern running shoe itself may be the major cause of running injuries! Stated another way, the modern running shoe, presently thought of a protective device, should be reclassified as a "health hazard." (NIKE, please tell me it ain't so!!!)

Now relax, get back on your chair and take a deep breath. We'll take this one step at a time and since we're going to be talking about shoes and feet, I may as well start at the beginning ... the very beginning. Until quite recently in our history, most humans lived out their lives unshod. S.F. Stewart in his "Footgear—Its History, Uses and Abuses" states that " ... all writers who have reported their observations of barefoot peoples agree that the untrammeled feet of natural men are free from the disabilities commonly noted among shod people—hallux valgus, bunions, hammer toe and painful feet."

So why was footgear developed? One of the earliest examples of footgear known to us takes the form of sagebrush bark sandals found in caves and rock shelters near Fort Rock, Oregon under a layer of volcanic ash dating back 10,000 years. The foot surface is smooth and they were held on by bast straps over the instep. Similar sandals were used throughout the volcanic cordilleras of Meso and South America and the volcanic islands of the South Pacific. The early Polynesians used sandals to cross old lava flows and when fishing on the razor-sharp coral. It seems, therefore, that the prime function of the earliest sandals was protection of the sole.

Although the early Pharaohs are all represented as barefoot, by the first millennium BC sandals in Egypt were common in court and were worn by soldiers. In Mesopotamian kingdoms sandals were evidently a status symbol with the king known to have worn a wedged sandal in contrast to his flat-soled courtiers. Very thick-soled low boots are known to have been worn by Greek tragedians to increase their height. Comedians wore socks or soccus—hence the expression "high tragedy and low comedy." Thus, the secondary function of footgear appears to have been symbolic.

From the time of the Greeks, footgear gradually evolved to meet both symbolic and functional needs. For example, tradition tells us that about the beginning of the present millennium Count Fulk of Anjou introduced long, pointed toes to cover up some deformity of his feet, and courtiers quickly adopted the fashion. The Mongols, who on horseback ravaged the Middle East between Damascus and Moscow from the 12th to 14th centuries, are credited for the introduction of the block heel presumably developed to better grip the stirrup plate. But in the French court of Louis XIV, the rugged Mongolian heel underwent a radical cosmetic transformation eventually leading to the ultimate idiotic expression of modern fashion—the stiletto heel.

European peasants wore clogs carved from a block of wood. Mass production seems to have begun prior to the 14th century, for Edward II in 1342 decreed that shoes should be sized. Their length was measured in barleycorns, three to an inch. This is still the basis of shoe measurements, one-third inch to a size in length. We start sizing from a baseline of three inches in children and seven inches in adults. Widths vary with length; in a given size the widths vary by one and a half inches. Unpaired shoes were introduced in England in the 15th century when gout became common and these shoes had broad square toes to relieve pressure. The most recent innovation seems to have been the hard box toe to preserve the appearance of the shoe.

Now, let's focus in on the running shoe. It seems that the earliest sports shoes were developed in the 1830s by the Liverpool rubber company owned by John Boyd Dunlop. Although they were first called sand shoes because they were worn on the beach by the Victorian middle classes, they eventually became known as plimsolls because the lines formed by the rubber and canvas bond looked similar to the Plimsoll line on a ship's hull. In 1933, Dunlop launched its Green Flash range of trainers. Adi Dassler (and his brother Rudolf) started making sports shoes in Herzogenaurach, Germany in 1920 and in 1936 Jesse Owens wore a pair of them when he won four Olympic gold medals in Berlin. ADIDAS (Adi Dassler) was formed in 1948 with the now famous three stripes logo developing from three support leather bands used to bolster the sides. By the 1956 Olympics, dozens of competitors were wearing ADIDAS shoes. Rudolf Dassler broke away to form PUMA. Amidst the first rumblings of the jogging boom, NIKE (after the Greek goddess of victory) was launched by American Phil Knight, a former track star at the University of Oregon, and his waffle-making coach Bill Bowerman in 1971(Surely you remember the NIKE Waffle Trainer!). The NIKE 'Swoosh' is arguably the most successful logo in the world and was conceived for Phil Knight by a local Oregon graphic design student, Carolyn Davidson, for a total fee of $35. (But don't worry about the graphic designer. In September 1983, NIKE presented Carolyn Davidson with a rather substantial share package as a way of saying "Thank-you.") ASICS (acronym for Animus Sanus In Corpore Sano, which is Latin for A Sound Mind In A Sound Body) first introduced its shoes in North America in 1977 while REEBOK (named after a species of an African gazelle) entered the U.S. Market in 1979 as the running shoe was slowly transforming into a fashion item. Eight years later, 1987 was declared the "Year of the Running Shoe" by the clothing industry, the same year NIKE launched the "cross-trainer" and its flagship running-shoe, the Air Max. After 16 years of research, NIKE introduced its SHOX line of runners in 2000, arguably the first athletic shoe on springs (foam)!

Part 2—Shoes and Injuries

For the last 15 years or so, buying a pair of runners has always been accompanied by a warm fuzzy feeling inside, a feeling that comes from the certain knowledge that you're investing in a high-tech device purpose-designed to protect you from injury and improve your performance. You can just see all those smart dedicated NIKE mechanical engineers hard at work developing and testing newer and better space-age materials to shield you from the terrible pounding you submit yourself to in order to "Just do it!' Gel, air, channels, honeycomb, microspheres, super-light materials, foam springs and soon ... yes, you guessed it, micro-chips in the soles of your shoes (better than diamonds, I suppose). New round laces and ribbon eyelets result in that custom-fitted feel supplemented by molded sorbothane insoles or special orthotics from your local prosthetist and you're ready to tackle any distance.

Now here's the catch. If all this high-tech stuff is supposed to be preventing running injuries by shielding us from impact, why is it that two out of every three runners are sidelined every year because of a running injury? Why is it that since the great jogging boom of the mid-seventies, there has been no decrease in the incidence (some authors say there has been an increase) of running injures in spite of yearly 'improvements' in running-shoe technology? Why is my office filled with runners who have injured knees (26% of running injuries), tibias (13%), Achilles tendons (6%) and plantar fascias (5%)? The cause of all these injuries is quite evident: cumulative micro-trauma caused by repetitive impact experienced during running. The heel of a runner upon striking the ground generates a force that can equal 2.5 times body weight at the foot and as much as 7 times body weight at the hip. Repeat this 1000 times per mile and it's easy to appreciate the stress the old bones are under. Add to this the hardness of urban roadways compared to naturally deposited surfaces and eventually, something gives, inflammation sets in and pain results ... and you end up working at the finish-line pulling bar-codes off finishers. Now, where's our high-tech shoe in all this? With all the improvements in recent years, you'd think we'd be seeing a marked decrease in running injuries. Just keep reading.

It wasn't till the mid-eighties that some researchers smelled something rotten in the athletic footwear world and it wasn't just dirty socks. Footwear manufacturers were well aware that impact was the cause of running injuries and reasoned that the way to attenuate impact was to interpose a soft impact-absorbing midsole between the foot and the ground. The first major problem was the method used by essentially all the footwear development labs to test the impact absorption of footwear mid-soles. Dr. Benno Nigg from the University of Calgary showed that machine testing of these materials by dropping a 5-kg object onto the shoe-sole and measuring the impact on a pressure-plate did not accurately predict human impact with the same materials. In fact the correlation turned out to be inverse, that is when you drop a 5-kg ball on materials of increasing softness, you measure decreasing impact. However, when the impact from a running human is measured, the result is the reverse, and the impact increases with softer materials! WHOOPS! (You'll find out why later.)

Next problem. In 1989, Dr. B. Marti published a paper which still makes the throats of footwear executives go dry. He studied 5,038 runners who participated in a 16K race and had them fill out an extensive questionnaire about their running in the year preceding the race. Here's what he found: The incidence of injuries in runners using shoes costing more than $95 was more than twice as great as in runners using shoes costing less than $40. (Note that this result includes correction for other influencing factors such as training mileage and history of previous injury.) In other words, the fancier (high-tech, advanced) the shoe, the more dangerous it is! Now a study of over 5,000 runners is not something to thumb your nose at and you would think the shoe manufacturers would have taken some notice. Not on your life. Yearly athletic shoe sales were in the billions of dollars and this was no time to fiddle with a successful product. In any case, it is felt by many observers that by the mid-eighties researchers, in-house or independent, had effectively been forced out of the loop of new product development and that research and development was now exclusively in the hands of the marketing people. Athletic shoes had become a fashion item and were designed as such, as they are to this day.

The big question: Why are super shock-absorbing athletic shoes causing more running injuries? Dr. Steven Robbins from the Centre for Studies in Aging at McGill University in Montreal is the man who came up with the answer. Dr. Robbins pointed out that the human lower extremity is not a delicate, rigid, passive structure

requiring 'packaging' to protect it from impact. This becomes bla-
tantly obvious when one observes the nearly complete absence
of foot disorders in unshod populations. People who go around
barefoot just don't get plantar fasciitis or any of the other lower
extremity injuries so common in shod populations. The lower extremity, he points out, is a rugged, flexible, active, well-designed
(teleologically) structure. Wire this structure to a spinal cord and
a brain and what you've got is a system fully capable of handling
the impacts of running. So, how does this system work exactly
and why do modern running shoes screw it up?

Allow me for a moment to compare the human locomotor ap-
paratus to a modern luxury car. The bones of the foot, leg, thigh
and pelvis act as the frame, linked by joints and all held together
by fairly inelastic ligaments and fascia. The bones and joints are
surrounded by contracting muscles which act as the suspension
system. This is especially evident in the arch of the
foot which is formed by both the passive, rigid plantar fascia as
well as the active, flexible intrinsic muscles. The bones and muscles are covered by fat and skin within which reside receptors or
sensors that send information to both the peripheral computer
(the spinal cord) and the central computer (the brain). The skin
on the sole of the foot (glabrous skin) is very well suited to its
function possessing about 600% of the toughness of hairy skin
(the skin everywhere else on our bodies except our palms). The
receptors in the foot are specially designed to sense both impact
(vertical force) and shear (horizontal force). Add to this information streaming in from pain receptors as well as joint position
receptors throughout the lower extremity and you've got a Hum-
mer! (Got carried away a little ... sorry.)

During barefoot running, the ball of the foot strikes the ground
first and immediately starts sending signals to the spinal cord
and brain about the magnitude of impact and shear, getting most
of its clues about this from the skin contact with the surface irregularities of the ground. Take away this contact by adding a
cushioned substance and you immediately fool the system into
underestimating the impact. Add a raised heel and the shod runner is forced to land on it. Strap the cushioning on tightly with the
aid of a sophisticated lacing system and you block out shear as
well, throwing the shock-absorption system even further into the
dark. The system responds by landing harder in an attempt to
compress the cushion and 'feel' the ground. The weight is then

transferred to the outside edge of the foot, completely by-passing the skin of the arch. The heel then touches down and the weight is transferred to the ball again with final push-off through the toes. While the weight is being transferred, the arch carries out its function as the suspension system of the foot and flattens under the active control of the intrinsic muscles. The ankle, knee and hip joints flex to absorb impact in response to information flowing in from the foot. The cushioned midsole of the modern running shoe robs the system of important sensory information necessary for ankle, knee and hip response to impact. The arch support (or orthotic) in modern running shoes not only prevents the arch suspension system from absorbing energy by preventing flattening but eventually leads to intrinsic muscle atrophy and complete loss of active muscular control of the arch leaving only the inelastic plantar fascia as a checkrein to flattening. The barefoot runner's 'foot position awareness sense' which relies heavily on sensory input from the sole of the foot minimizes his risk of sustaining an ankle sprain on uneven ground. The shod runner is at marked increased risk of ankle sprains because his 'foot position awareness sense' is handicapped by the paucity of sensations coming from his soles. The barefoot runner is constantly alert scanning the ground before him for irregularities and dangers that might cause him injury. The barefoot runner is a cautious runner and actively changes his landing strategy to prevent injury. He treads lightly. The shod runner is bombarded by convincing advertising stating or implying that the shoe he is wearing will protect him well over any terrain and he becomes a careless runner. He is heavy footed. Finally, certain diseases in humans can cause a gradual destruction of the sensory nerve endings in the foot (and elsewhere) resulting in a significant increase in lower extremity injuries. Diabetes and tertiary syphilis are two. Extremities so affected are termed 'neuropathic'. The shod runner, because of his sensory deprivation and high risk of injury may be termed as having 'pseudo-neuropathic' feet, a term coined by Robbins.

The conclusion that shoes are the primary cause of running injuries is strongly supported by the scientific literature. I've already mentioned Marti's work showing more than twice the incidence of running injuries with expensive shoes compared with cheap ones. Rao and Joseph (1992) examined 2300 Indian children between the ages of 4 and 13 and found that the incidence of flat feet was more than three times greater in those children who used footwear than in those who did not leading them to conclude that shoe-wearing in early childhood is detrimental to the development of a normal arch. In 1988, Hamill and Bates showed that as running shoes lose their cushioning through wear and tear, subjects improve foot control on testing and presumably decrease their risk of injury, i.e. shoes get better with age. Robbins and Gouw showed in 1991 that modern athletic footwear creates a perceptual illusion in subjects whereby they consistently underestimate impact. Simply adding surface irregularities on the insoles (to simulate barefoot like conditions) markedly improves subjects' estimates of impact. Robbins and others (1994) studied the balance ability of men walking along a beam wearing shoes with soles of varying thickness and hardness. Results confirmed that the thinner and harder the soles, the better the balance. In one of their most elegant and widely publicized studies, Robbins and Waked (1997) examined the effect of advertising on landing impact. They asked subjects to step down barefoot ten times onto four pressure-measuring platforms, the first one being bare and the other three covered by identical shoe sole material made to look different by different colored cloth. The subjects were given different messages for each of the covered plates: the message for the first covered plate suggested superior impact absorption and protection (deceptive message), the second suggested poor impact absorption and high injury risk (warning message) and the third suggested unknown impact absorption and safety (neutral message). Results showed that subjects landed with the highest impact when given the deceptive and neutral messages and with the lowest impact when given the warning message or with the bare plate. The authors conclude that running injury rates are greatest in users of the most expensive shoes because advertising has deceived these users into believing that the shoes provide a superior level of safety thereby inducing an attenuation of impact moderating behavior, increasing impact and injury. The authors add that deceptive advertising of protective devices is a public health hazard and should be addressed. Humans are less cautious even when they use truthfully advertised products because of excessively positive attitudes toward new products and wrong impressions of the standards of truth in advertising.

"So," you think, "is this guy telling me that NIKE, REEBOK and all those big corporations just put this new stuff out on the market without any proof that its safe? Can't be!" Well, that's exactly what I'm telling you. I can be a real pain in the ass when I try, and some years back, I was in the mood. I got on the phone and tried to talk to the directors of research at all the big athletic footwear companies. I tell you, getting to talk to one of these guys is harder than talking to the Pope. I finally got to speak with Mr. Gordon Valiant, then director of research at the NIKE Sports Research Lab in Beaverton, Oregon.

JF: "Mr. Valiant. My name is Dr. Froncioni and I'm an orthopedic surgeon. I treat a lot of runners and I was just wondering what your thoughts were on the whole issue of running injuries possibly being caused by your running shoes."

... long pause ...

GV: "Umm ... well ... I'm afraid I'm not at liberty to discuss that matter."

SAY WHAT!!!??

JF: "Mr. Valiant, in case you missed it, I'm NOT a reporter. I'm just an orthopedic surgeon who's looking for some answers for his patients. Let me rephrase. Surely you have data to support the injury protection claims you make about your running shoes ... surely sir ... "

GV: "Well ... I could refer you to our marketing people and I'm sure they could send you something."

Nope. We're not on the same wavelength at all. I'm sure the lawyers have given these guys a gag order.

JF: "Mr.Valiant, your marketing people send me stuff all the time; it's all over the *Runner's World* I get every month. Anyway, nice talking to you."

I've also had a few chats with Dr. Steven Robbins. He feels very strongly that the athletic footwear manufacturers are painting themselves into a very tight corner by not acting on the available information. After all, it is within their power to effect changes in their shoe design based on the available data and in doing so decreasing the running injury rate by up to 55%. By not acting now, Dr. Robbins predicts the footwear manufacturers may end up in the same situation as the tobacco companies with massive class-action lawsuits brought against them.

Part 3—New Directions

So, what do we do now? For starters, NO, I do not recommend that you run your next half-marathon barefoot. But certainly, I predict that sooner or later, changes will come about in both shoe design and training. From the medical establishment's point of view, the prevention and treatment of running injuries must change to incorporate the concepts outlined above. In fact I view the ideas I've presented here as a major paradigm shift in sports medicine, the likes of which I have not seen in the last fifteen years. Of course, the major shoe companies have to own up and start introducing better shoes into their lines. Why not do this gradually and introduce just one shoe that incorporates some of the recommended changes. Dr. Robbins is already testing shoes that use a thinner, less resilient midsole material that provides the comfort but not the impact absorption and of course has no arch support. I'm sure the marketing boys at NIKE could handle it.

Without being too radical, there are some changes that are worth introducing without further delay and they are as follows:

1. Young children should be encouraged to spend as much time as possible barefoot. We know that this is especially important for the proper formation of the foot arch in the first six years of life. So, moms, trash the WEEBOKS and let your kids develop strong healthy feet just as they were meant to.

2. Runners should consider incorporating sessions of barefoot running into their training. In an article in the October 1997 *Runner's World*, Adam Bean gives the following advice: "Running barefoot a couple of times per week can decrease your risk of injury and boost your 'push-off' power." You can run on any surface you like as long as you're careful of sharp objects and pebbles. Soft sand is probably the least desirable surface because it is unstable and after your heel has dug-in, you will weight bear on your arch. Paved roads are fine and dangerous objects are easy to spot. But remember, your feet will need to toughen-up so start

with small doses. Kick your shoes off as soon as you get home and spend your evenings and weekends barefoot.

Is it possible to rehabilitate the weakened muscles of a normally shod runner? It certainly is according to another excellent study by Dr. Robbins (1987). He asked 17 normally shod recreational runners to gradually increase barefoot activity both at home and outdoors over a period of several weeks and to maintain barefoot activity for about four months. The runners' feet were examined, measured and x-rayed at regular intervals to detect changes. Results showed marked improvement in the anatomy and function of the arch. The authors concluded that the normally shod foot is capable of rehabilitation of foot musculature. Very good news indeed for all of us.

3. Runners may want to consider switching to a lightweight shoe that provides less cushioning and no arch support. The only shoes on the market that come close to these characteristics are racing flats. I use the 6.5 oz. ASICS Gel-Magic Racer. For you diehard NIKE fans, consider the Air Streak II, Air Streak Spectrum Plus or the Air Streak Vapor IV. But most shoe manufacturers make a flat. A shoe that Nike has just introduced this year, the NIKE FREE also looks like a step in the right direction (I have not actually seen this shoe myself yet). Moreover, a look at the NIKE FREE web page gives me a bit of hope that this company may finally have seen the light. If you do change to flats, I recommend you wean into them slowly. Remember that you live in a developed country and that your feet have been shielded from natural stresses your entire life, i.e. you've got wimpy feet, buddy. The intrinsic muscles of your feet are asleep and need to wake up slowly. The first thing that will strike you in a racing flat is the lightness of the shoe (Most runners today run in shoes that weigh as much as 14 oz.) Then, you will quickly realize that for the first time, you start to feel the ground you are walking on. Oh—and one more thing: don't listen to the guy at the running store. He's there to sell shoes and is under the spell of the powerful shoe industry advertising machine. He has become well and truly brainwashed with the

traditional concepts that we all need cushioning and arch support. He will try to dissuade you from buying a racing flat and he may even go as far as telling you that they are for elite runners and are meant to be used for one marathon only. Don't believe him. I keep my flats for at least 400–500 miles with no problem.

Finally, some radicals among you may wish to become full-time barefoot runners. Barefoot running clubs are springing-up all over America and Europe. Point your search engine to 'barefoot running' or go to www.runningbarefoot.org to get more information. I also welcome anyone who wishes more information on any of the quoted materials to contact me and it would be my pleasure to provide you with copies (josephfroncioni@logic.bm).

Joseph Froncioni

Understanding Basic Barefoot Running Terminology

Just to make sure there is an understanding of the various terms used in this book, here are some helpful tips on basic barefoot running terminology.

The term barefoot running is sometimes misused. Within the barefoot running community, *barefoot running* refers to running without any sort of shoe, sock, tape, or other foot covering.

On the other hand, *minimalist shoe running* refers to running with a shoe that provides little or no support, a very thin extremely flexible heel, and more or less allows the foot to operate in a natural way.

Reduced shoe running refers to running in shoes that have some support, a thicker sole, and a heel that may be slightly higher than the midfoot area.

Shod running refers to running in traditional running shoes that contain thick soles, lots of cushioning, and may provide a good deal of support for the foot and ankle.

The Barefoot Running Movement

The barefoot and minimalist shoe movement can be divided into various categories or factions. These divisions are predominantly based on perspective and theoretical differences. It is common for barefoot and minimalist shoe runners to shift from one group to another based on their own experiences or conditions.

The "barefoot purist" group: This group of barefoot runners will run exclusively barefoot and will shun shoes whenever possible—even minimal shoes. The theory is based on the idea that any shoe will interfere with the body's ability to run effectively.

The "shoes as tools" group: This group has the same theoretical perspective as the purists but will accept the use of minimalist shoes when conditions warrant—such as extreme weather or terrain.

The "minimalist shoe" group: This group generally agrees with the benefits of barefoot running but will rarely run barefoot, instead opting for minimalist shoes. In so doing they reject the importance of sensory feedback from the soles of the feet as a critical element of developing good running form.

Each of these groups will identify themselves as barefoot runners. Though the groups sometime disagree, all three groups share the common goal of helping people run in a more efficient manner with fewer injuries.

Is Barefoot Running a Fad?

A fad is defined as a temporary fashion, notion, or manner of conduct that is enthusiastically followed by a group. Until recently, barefoot running was an obscure practice followed by a tiny group of dedicated individuals—often labeled "crazy hippies" by our running brethren. This is now changing due to several events.

First, the peer-reviewed research began to make headlines as it became increasingly clear that the modern running shoe was not meeting the needs of all runners. Some advances in shoe technology may even have had a negative impact on the health of runners leading some members of the medical and running community to question the logic of the modern running shoe. So far this skepticism has had a relatively small impact on the running community.

The second major event was the release of the book *Born to Run* by Christopher McDougall. In his book, McDougall presents a convincing argument in support of minimalist shoes and barefoot running. The popularity of the book has spawned an enthusiasm that creates the perception for some that this movement is a fad or temporary craze.

Personally, I do not believe it. Certainly not a fad like leg warmers or river-dancing. Neither of which were supported by research. That said, I do not think barefoot running will ever surpass the popularity of shod running. Rather, I believe the movement will pressure shoe manufacturers to examine the research and development of their current shoes more critically resulting in moving away from the supportive and cushioned technology so prevalent today.

While some will choose to run barefoot a majority of the time—the "fun factor" alone will assure that—instead I believe the majority of runners will opt for a more conservative approach and make the switch to more minimal shoes. Barefoot running is a movement that will eventually help all of us to become healthier runners.

There will always be skeptics that question the logic of the barefoot/minimalist movement and many runners that have no history of injury caused by using cushioned, supportive shoes. Those runners should continue running as they have previously with occasional barefoot running as a healthy supplement to their normal training routine.

Personally, I believe the true benefits of barefoot running are the result of a more conservative training plan coupled with improved form. When beginning barefoot running, most runners will start at very low mileage and gradually build to longer and faster distances. This helps prevent "too much too soon" or over-use injuries. Barefoot running requires good form. The better your form, the less stress on your body resulting in fewer injuries.

Fear not, unless you are interested in barefoot running for the enjoyment factor, there is no need to completely abandon your shoes. Runners will receive some benefits of barefoot running even from a single unshod mile each week. If you are one of these runners, this book will provide tools that will be useful to you, even if you decide to forego barefoot or minimalist shoe running.

Do I Have to Run Barefoot?

While I would recommend barefoot running for all runners, it is not necessary to run barefoot full-time. In fact, running in minimalist or even reduced running shoes will provide many of the same benefits of barefoot running. There is research being conducted to determine exactly what causes the benefits of barefoot running though many speculate the relaxed, midfoot gait is primarily responsible for its positive effects.

Based on anecdotal evidence, minimalist shoe running is a healthier alternative to traditional cushioned motion-control running shoes. In essence, minimalist shoes help the foot work as it was intended to work. The more minimalistic a shoe design is, the greater benefit to the runner.

I recommend all runners learn to run barefoot prior to adding minimalist shoes to their training routine. Learning to run barefoot first will allow you to learn good form and strengthen your feet, legs, and other anatomy to help prevent injuries. While it is possible to learn to run in minimalist shoes first, the lack of tactile sensation with the ground will interfere with the process. Being able to feel the ground is a valuable training tool.

There are other excellent methods to help you learn to run with efficiency. Good Form Running®, Evolution Running®, ChiRunning®, and Pose® are four such methods. All four use slightly different methods to teach similar skills. Once you have learned good form through barefoot running, it can be beneficial to study each of these four methods. Each contains drills and exercises that you can use for experimentation. My own running form is a hybrid of my own experimentation coupled with elements from each of those four methods.

Recently Dr. Scott Hadley, founder of TrekoClinics.com, summed up the reasons for and history behind barefoot/minimalist running in his article titled, "This is Your Body on Shock: stretch reflexes, shock absorption, and barefoot/minimalist running." That article, used with his permission, follows:

In 1898, a neurophysiologist named William Sherrington published his findings on stretch reflexes. The basic idea of a stretch reflex is this: when a muscle is lengthened rapidly, a signal is sent to the central nervous system which triggers that muscle to contract. The "knee jerk" reflex is one example that you have probably seen when your doctor hits your knee with a little rubber hammer. The rapid stretch of the quads triggers a reflex that causes the muscle to contract—and the knee jerks.

In 1956, another neurophysiologist name J.C. Eccles reported that the stretch of one muscle not only causes reflex activation of that muscle, but other muscles are activated too. Eccles thus defined two types of stretch reflexes. A homonymous stretch reflex occurs when the stretch of a muscle causes that muscle to contract. A heteronymous stretch reflex occurs when the stretch of a muscle causes a different muscle to contract.

During the past 60 years, heteronymous stretch reflexes have been investigated extensively by neurophysiologists. Through surface EMG recordings in human subjects, dozens of heteronymous reflex patterns have been identified. It is thought that these reflexes allow the central nervous system to monitor and control gait and other complex human movements at an automatic, subconscious level.

Essentially, our body movements are in large part controlled by a series of stretch reflexes between muscles. When walking and running, the nervous system reads 'stretch information' from several key muscles and uses that information to activate or inactivate other muscles in a coordinated sequence. This is how we can walk, run, and perform other complex movements without thinking about it.

Let me give you a few examples of the role of stretch reflexes during running. When the foot hits the ground (initial contact), the first muscle to contract is the soleus of the calf—if you are landing properly without a heel strike. Forward momentum causes the soleus to stretch rapidly, and the soleus reflexively contracts to prevent the knee from buckling. While the soleus contracts, it also lengthens to allow the knee to advance over the foot (this is called an eccentric muscle contraction for you physiology buffs). Stretch reflexes from the lengthening soleus act as a powerful neurological switch that activates the quadriceps and hip extensors to prevent the leg and trunk from collapsing under the forces of landing on one foot. In fact, if the soleus doesn't stretch properly, the hip extensors can be up to 75% weaker due to a lack of heteronymous reflexive control.

The muscles in the bottom of the foot (the foot intrinsics) also play a role as body weight is accepted onto the foot. The foot intrinsics begin undergoing a lengthening (eccentric) contraction as the arch of the foot flattens slightly to absorb shock. The stretch reflexes initiated from the lengthening of the foot intrinsics produce an interesting mechanism of shock absorption at the knee and ankle by inhibiting the soleus and quadriceps—causing partial relaxation of these muscles—to allow the ankle and knee to give-way slightly as body weight is loaded onto the leg.

If the foot arch is over-supported by an orthotic or a motion-control shoe, the foot intrinsics are incapable of inhibiting the soleus and quadriceps. At a phase in the gait cycle where the soleus and quadriceps should be slightly more elastic to absorb shock, they remain more rigid, thus reducing shock absorption and causing excessive strain on the soleus, quadriceps, and joint structures. Over time, if the arch is over-supported, the foot intrinsics become weak and are no longer effective. The foot intrinsics become weak and tight, stretch reflexes become inhibited, muscles do not 'turn on' when they need to, and biomechanics break down. The end result is overuse injury—something most runners experience at some point.

But barefoot and minimalist running allows the foot arch to deform naturally, allowing the stretch reflexes from the foot intrinsics to activate a very effective shock absorption mechanism. It's almost counterintuitive that running barefoot or in minimalist shoes produces less impact than running in supportive, padded running shoes. But research has shown just that. And the stretch reflexes from muscles in the foot are partially responsible for this.

Since the foot intrinsics are used more in barefoot and minimalist running, we invariably go through a phase of muscle soreness and growth of the foot intrinsics and soleus during the transition out of standard running shoes and after a long run. But rejoice in your aching foot muscles! This is your body absorbing shock as nature intended.

Scott Hadley, Ph.D, DPT
©2010 TrekoClinics.com

Can I Still Maintain My High Mileage and Learn to Run Barefoot on the Side?

The best way to learn barefoot running is to start from scratch. However, experienced runners often have difficulty stopping their high mileage training. This is understandable; we do have an addictive hobby! If you are currently training and are unwilling to restart from zero mileage, there is a solution. Note: this solution does present some potential risks and common problems.

If you do wish to continue your normal shod training, I would recommend adding all drills and running in place of some of your current cross training or running activities. For example, if you currently run 50 miles per week try running three miles barefoot and 47 miles shod. Then slowly, over time, replace your shod miles with barefoot miles. If running in minimalist shoes is your goal, it is best to learn barefoot running first and then switch to minimalist shoes. Once you learn proper barefoot form, you can exchange the barefoot mileage with minimalist shoe mileage.

The most common problem that arises with this plan occurs after you start to develop good barefoot form. Increasingly it will become difficult to run in traditional shoes. Your feet will begin to feel incredibly heavy and the rest of your body will rebel against the pounding as you start to crave the gentle smoothness of barefoot or minimalist shoe running. This usually happens well before you are ready to convert all of your training mileage to barefoot or minimalist shoe mileage. The result is usually a temporary decrease in training mileage as you abandon your traditional shoes. You will quickly regain the mileage, but that reduction in training can be stressful for some. There are other activities that can be done as a substitute, such as weight training, swimming, or aerobics.

Minimalist Shoe Recommendations?

Sometimes people will ask for a minimalist shoe recommendation. It is difficult to recommend one particular shoe, because each individual will have particular tastes. Personally I have a strong preference for shoes that allow my feet to operate as if I were barefoot. For me, there are a few important qualities every minimalist shoe must have:

• *Flat, thin, flexible sole*—This is the most important aspect of any minimalist shoe. The heel must be the same thickness as the forefoot area. A raised heel will alter your gait making it nearly impossible to run as if you were barefoot while a thin sole allows for greater "ground feel," or the ability of the tactile sensory cells in the sole of your feet to feel the terrain under foot. The flexible sole allows the foot to move more or less unencumbered.

• *Wide toe box*—This allows the toes to splay, or spread out, when your foot kisses the ground. This physical sensation is part of a complex neural reflex that seems to facilitate good running form. Research on this concept is in its infancy.

• *Lightweight, flexible upper*—Of the three qualities, this is least important. Oddly, most "traditional" shoe manufacturers seem to place more importance on the upper than the sole or toe box. Still, a lightweight flexible upper will allow the shoe to move with your foot.

The market for minimalist shoes is rapidly expanding as both new and older shoe manufacturers rush to meet the demands of our growing ranks. The following companies produce shoes I would recommend:

• *Merrell®* (http://merrell.com)—Merrell® is a brand within Wolverine World Wide Inc.'s Outdoor Group. Merrell believes in encouraging everyone to get outside, be active and have fun. To help drive this mission, in 2011 Merrell introduced an entire collection of barefoot shoes to "let your feet lead you" into your barefoot adventure of choice. In collaboration with Vibram®, the world leader in advanced sole design, Merrell Barefoot is the perfect balance of barefoot essential insight, fit and feel, with a zero heel to toe drop and super light, low profile that connect feet to any outdoor terrain. www.merrell.com.

facebook—www.facebook.com/merrell

twitter—twitter.com/merrelloutside

As of 2011, Merrell's Trail Glove barefoot-inspired shoes are my personal favorites. Merrell managed to combine all of the characteristics of my ideal minimalist shoe into one package. The fit and function of the shoe is second to none. This is the shoe I use for running ultramarathons. If I were to give a single recommendation, this shoe would be it.

• *Terra Plana VivoBarefoot®* (www.terraplana.com)—In 2004, Terra Plana became pioneers of the barefoot movement by launching its first minimalist shoe collection with a mission to make footwear that offers all the health benefits of being barefoot with the protection of shoes. Today, as the research to support barefoot health grows, so does the collection. They now offer a total lifestyle solution for the whole family. Their goal is not only to spread the word and forward the barefoot movement, but also to educate how to transition properly. They understand that the body is a biomechanical masterpiece with the foot as its showpiece. No heel, no midsole, no arch support, no gimmicks, VivoBarefoot works with the body not against it—allowing the foot to be as millions of years of evolution intended ... barefoot. All VivoBarefoot products are eco-friendly and sustainable. They use recycled, locally-sourced materials in efficient production processes at independently monitored factories. Priding themselves on being good for the body and kind to the environment.

• *Luna Sandals®* (http://lunasandals.com)—Luna Sandal Company is interested in the designs of traditional sandals from all over the world, sandals made out of natural, sustainable materials that are easy to make by hand with simple tools. Luna believe that the minimalist footwear traditions are part of our shared heritage and that we should preserve them and encourage others to do the same. The Luna sandal collection represents the best fruits of their experiences and experiments with old-school footwear and gleanings from insights that they have gathered from both our ancestors and their customers. Through small-scale, sustainable production, they give a growing audience a chance to try what they consider to be fine minimalist running sandals that happen to be great everyday footwear too.

• *Vibram*® (http://vibram.com)—Vibram's Five Fingers line is the most popular minimalist shoe line. I used a "KSO" model when running a 100-miler. Their "Trek" model remains one of my favorites. Vibram also understands what constitutes good minimalist shoes. I would highly recommend any shoe from their line.

• *Inov-8*® (http://www.inov-8.com/)—Our philosophy is to design product around the natural function of the human body's biomechanics. We look to the body's innate movement for inspiration and guidance. The human foot is perfectly adapted to accommodate variations in ground orientation and, with each step, changes its mechanical characteristics from a flexible adaptive platform to a rigid propulsive lever. Whatever the terrain, however far over the horizon you intend to run, inov-8 footwear works in synergy with the natural biomechanics of the body, allowing the foot to do what it does best. Each inov-8™ shoe protects the foot, providing the wearer with a secure and intimate fit that's almost like running barefoot.

• *Feelmax*® (http://feelmax.com)—Feelmax is a company based in Finland. I do not personally have a lot of experience with their shoes, but they are among the favorites of barefoot runners.

• *Soft Star*® (www.softstarshoes.com)—Soft Star is a small company that produces moccasins. They recently developed a running moccasin called the "RunAmoc." The concept behind the moccasin is precisely what I would define as the ideal minimalist shoe.

• *Kigo*® (www.kigofootwear.com)—Kigo footwear is stylish, eco-friendly minimalist footwear for barefoot athletics and everyday wear. The kigo team strives to provide comfortable shoes that are stylish enough for everyday wear, sturdy enough for athletics and constructed to be as good for the earth as for the body. Each kigo shoe is thoughtfully and responsibly constructed of lightweight eco-friendly materials, including removable EVA insoles, breathable, stain/water resistant uppers and flexible, high-density rubber outsoles.

• *Invisible Shoe*® (www.invisibleshoe.com)—Invisible Shoe produces custom-made huarache running sandals. They also sell kits that allow you to make your own. Huaraches are one of my personal favorite minimalist running shoes. I use Invisible Shoe exclusively for huaraches.

• *Sockwa*® (www.sockwa.com)—Sockwa began as a company that produced shoes for beach soccer. Their product line now includes shoes that are ideal for minimalist running.

• *Newton*® (www.newtonrunning.com)—Newton does not produce minimalist shoes. Rather, they produce shoes with little or no heel-to-toe differential, but still maintain the qualities of a traditional running shoe. The major advantage to Newton shoes is they allow you to run with excellent form while still maintaining great protection and cushioning.

There are a few other small companies such as Sanuk®, Stem, Altra, and ZEM that produce true minimalist shoes. Also, some of the major shoe manufacturers are beginning to produce more pseudo-minimalist shoes.

Among the "traditional" shoe manufacturers, Nike leads the way with their "Free" line. While I would classify the Free as a "reduced running shoe," Nike is beginning to incorporate better technology that allows the foot to move independently within the shoe.

Other companies like GoLite, Saucony, and Adidas are actively producing either reduced-running shoes or even true minimalist shoes.

Within the next couple years I predict the market will become flooded with a plethora of minimalist shoe options from all major shoe manufacturers. This competition for the minimalist shoe market should produce some excellent shoes that compliment the current offerings.

Minimalist shoes can be purchased at many local running stores. Most minimalist shoe manufacturers have a "store locator" function on their website and many are also available online. Among my favorite stores are Zombie Runner in Palo Alto, California (http://www.zombierunner.com), Gazelle Sports in West Michigan (http://gazellesports.com), and Two Rivers Treads in Shepardstown, West Virginia (http://www.trtreads.org.)

Plasti-Socks: The minimalist shoe alternative

Disappointed that some "minimal" footwear seemed to be moving further away from providing ground feedback, I decided to try making my own. One day while looking for a way to reinforce the bottom of a sock, I found someone online who had done just that, with an aerosol spray can of a product called Plasti-Dip.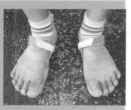

A trip to the hardware store, a little experimentation, and I easily made a nice pair of running socks with a thin rubberized sole. When the sole wears thin, they can easily be reinforced. Though I've been running mostly barefoot lately, I'm contemplating a winter barefoot solution. Perhaps wool plasti-socks?

Joel Wermiel
http://thewerm.com

My Guiding Principles

The following are the principles that guide my philosophy regarding barefoot running. These principles have been developed over time based on my personal experiences, studying the available research, observing other runners, and discussing barefoot running with peers.

Principle One: There is no single right answer.
Barefoot running is inherently a very individualistic activity. Each of us will develop our own style and form—there is no single "correct" way to run barefoot. Some pre-packaged techniques, such as ChiRunning, Good Form Running, Evolution Running, and the POSE method can be very effective methods to learn minimalist shoe or barefoot running. However, all methods take an "our way is the right way" approach which simply is not the case when running barefoot. None of them are the single best method for all runners. Therefore, my job as a teacher of barefoot running is to help you find your own style.

Principle Two: You must experiment and learn from your successes and failures.
George Sheehan famously said, "Each of us is an experiment of one-observer and subject-making choices, living with them, recording the effects." In order to master the art of running barefoot, you must be willing to try new things—adopting the successes and discarding the failures. I've used this concept to develop some truly unorthodox running habits such as eating hot dogs, Ben and Jerry's ice cream, and alcohol-based iskiate as race fuel, wearing cotton hoodies instead of the latest moisture-wicking fabrics, and actively seeking out rugged terrain to practice barefoot trail running skills.

Principle Three: Your body is your best teacher.
When following principle two, your best feedback will be your own body. Your brain has the amazing ability to receive

feedback from your body, interpret that information, and adjust accordingly. Our own thought processes often create roadblocks for this process. We must learn to trust what our own body is telling us. Feel, don't think. If we feel a shock with each step, we have to modify our form until the shock disappears. Your body is the most efficient running coach you can employ.

Principle Four: Patience is mandatory.
Learning to run barefoot takes time. Allowing your body to adapt to this new running style can be a slow journey. All too often we want to rush the process. This results in injury. You have likely spent a majority of your life wearing heavy shoes with raised heels. Like a broken arm that spends weeks in a cast, your feet will have grown weak. It takes time to build strength. You must be willing to start from nothing and rebuild yourself as a stronger runner.

Principle Five: Relaxation is the secret to great form.
Barefoot running requires relaxation of the skeletal muscles. Running free and easy is the secret to running injury-free. Your arms and legs should have about as much tension as a wet noodle. For "foodies," think well-cooked pasta, not al dente.

Principle Six: You must enjoy the process.
Learning to run barefoot should be a process, not a destination. If you take the time to enjoy each stage of your development as a barefoot runner, you will be successful. This is a fun activity! Watch little children run around barefoot. They know something most of us have long-since forgotten. Embrace that joy! Smile and savor the process!

Factors that Affect Speed of Transition

When learning to run barefoot, several factors will affect the speed at which you can make the transition from traditional shoes to barefoot or minimalist shoes. The greatest factor seems to be prior barefoot experience. Runners that routinely do other activities barefoot will be able to advance at a faster rate. Their muscles, tendons, ligaments, bones, and plantar skin will be more adept at the stresses and rigors of barefoot running.

Runners that have adopted a midfoot strike will also be able to advance faster. This particular running style is nearly identical to barefoot form. Like individuals that spend time barefoot, this group will have already pre-strengthened many of the anatomical features that are stressed when running barefoot.

Youth may play a role since younger runners are able to physically heal at a faster rate—thus progressing faster.

Prior injury history plays a role. Runners with few injuries may be able to advance at a faster rate.

A runner's ability to listen to their body will also make a difference. A key to learning good form is the ability to monitor the state of your body.

Finally, trail runners may be able to transition faster due to their already-developed skills of running on uneven surfaces and monitoring the terrain they are running.

All these factors may play a role in the rate of progression.

Regardless of your own characteristics, it is important to exercise patience. You will learn to run barefoot significantly faster if you utilize a "slow and steady" approach.

Listen To Your Body

It will tell you when you should slow down or when you're ready to speed up. It will tell you when you need to step lighter or when you can plow through some terrain. It will tell you when you are ready to increase your cadence or when you need to slow it down. It will tell you when you can go out and run again or when you need a little more time to recover from the last run. Learning to listen to your body is crucial in barefoot/minimalist running and experience will help in interpreting the messages.

Tina DuBois
http://toegirltina.blogspot.com/

Explanation of Concepts, Issues, and Activities

This book is organized using a progression of methods. It is important to master each stage before progressing to the next. The four stages are:

Pre-running: What to do before starting to run barefoot.
Starting to Run Barefoot: How to begin learning the fundamental skills needed to run barefoot.
Intermediate Barefoot Running: Increasing speed and/or distance; improving barefoot running skill.
Advanced Barefoot Running: Special issues such as racing, extreme weather, etc.

Each of the first three stages are comprised of:
Concepts, issues, and activities.

 Concepts are the major theories that constitute good barefoot running. They may include elements like form, frame of mind, or other important elements of learning to run barefoot.

 Issues are the problems or concerns that may arise when implementing the various activities that will teach you the skills of barefoot running.

 Activities are the various physical tasks you will practice to learn to run barefoot. The next section introduces some sample schedules based on some fictional individuals of varying experience.

Sample Training Schedule

To aid your progress in transitioning to barefoot or minimalist shoe running, I've provided a handy schedule. This schedule has been subject to several important revisions. The original aptly-named "Lose the Shoes" plan I developed was widely spread via the *Runner's World* Barefoot Running Forum and my own Barefoot Running University website. Many people successfully followed the plan. While effective, it was also very conservative. The rigid nature of the plan did not suit all runners' unique situations. The modified plan presented in this book utilizes the same principles, but allows enough flexibility for all runners.

On the following page are two sample plans that use this concept. The first plan is designed for a novice runner or a runner that would not be well-suited to quickly adapt to barefoot running. See "Factors that Affect Speed of Transition."

In this case the novice is a middle-age man I'll call Timmy, who has recently decided to start running. While in high school Timmy was an athlete but has since lapsed into a sedentary lifestyle. He wears shoes everywhere, as he has since childhood. It will be important for Timmy to start slow and spend extra time acclimating his feet to this foreign world without shoes.

Stage One—Pre-Running—2–3 weeks
Stage Two—Starting to Run Barefoot—3–4 weeks
Stage Three—Intermediate Barefoot Running—4–5 weeks
Stage Four—Advanced Barefoot Running—After 9–12 weeks

Janice is an experienced marathon runner in her mid-twenties. She has qualified for the Boston Marathon multiple times. Janice routinely spends a lot of time walking around barefoot, whether it be at home or at the beach. Lately she has been training on trails in preparation for an ultra-marathon. Since Janice has a strong background in barefoot activities and is young, she will not require the conservative plan Timmy required. The following would be an appropriate schedule for an individual such as Janice.

Stage One—Pre-Running—One week (to learn form)
Stage Two—Starting to Run Barefoot—2–3 weeks
Stage Three—Intermediate B arefoot Running—3–4 weeks
Stage Four—Advanced Barefoot Running—After 6–8 weeks

Regardless of the pace you set for yourself, it is important to follow the guidelines of only increasing distance by 10% per week or pace by 15 seconds per mile per week. This will prevent overuse injuries.

Pre-running
Before you run, you walk.

Learning to run barefoot or in minimalist shoes will put unusual stress on your body. After wearing traditional shoes for years, your lower anatomy is weak and unprepared to handle the workload of functioning in a way in which it was designed.

It is like wearing a cast for weeks or months. The underlying muscles atrophy and weaken. Because of this developed weakness, it takes some time to strengthen your body in preparation of running in a different way.

Also, other physiological adaptations must occur. The soles of your feet must adapt to the new-found freedom of feeling the ground under foot. Your brain has to reacquaint itself with interpreting the information being sent from sensory neurons in your feet. You have to develop some degree of foot-eye coordination and the habit of scanning the terrain you are walking or running through.

All too often, wearing shoes gives us a false sense of security. Thick shoes allow us to completely ignore everything surrounding our feet. It takes time to reawaken that spatial awareness. New barefoot runners often ask how to avoid stepping on broken beer bottles, hypodermic needles, or feces. Easy! You watch where you are going! This introductory stage will help accomplish these feats.

You may be tempted to jump into the actual running. Some people may be able to do just that. In the "Factors that Affect Speed of Transition" section, I discussed some of the factors that may allow some individuals to advance at a faster rate. Even if you believe you already have the skills and abilities necessary to skip this stage, I would highly recommend you spend at least a week or two contemplating the concepts and practicing the drills. It will better prepare you to progress through the more advanced stages.

You will be ready to advance to the next stage once you reach the following goals:

- Walk in place for five minutes without pain either during or after the activity.
- Feel comfortable with the feeling of lifting your feet off the ground versus "pushing off."
- Feel comfortable with your ability to relax all tension in your arms and legs.

Concept—Feel Instead of Think

 Barefoot running is inherently individualistic. It is impossible to give a detailed explanation of the perfect barefoot running form. Every barefoot runner will have a slightly different form that works best for their individual characteristics. Because of this, I will teach the basic components all barefoot runners have in common. It will be your responsibility to experiment to find out exactly what will work best for you.

Luckily, this is a relatively easy task. All you have to do is listen to your body. The soles of your feet are the best teachers you have and will transfer critical information to your brain. In turn, your brain will send a signal to your muscles to provide the smoothest, most efficient gait possible.

It is important to be able to simply feel and react to what you are experiencing. Thinking about the tiny details of your form tends to short-circuit this process. Because of this, I prefer to avoid explaining many details that must be remembered and processed while running. Instead, I will give you one or two concepts at a time, then give you the drills to practice them. My goal is to teach you proper barefoot form that is tailored to your individual characteristics in the most time-efficient way possible.

Concept—Importance of Patience

 Throughout the process of learning to run barefoot or in minimalist shoes, it is important to be patient. Your feet have likely spent many years encased in heavy, sweaty foot coffins (a term Barefoot Ted coined). Those shoes have weakened the muscles, tendons, ligaments, bones, and plantar skin of your feet and adjacent anatomy.

Because your feet have become used to shoes for so many years, I cannot emphasize enough the need for patience by slowly increasing your barefoot experiences.

In the beginning, you may be tempted to run farther than you should. In the barefoot running world, we refer to this as "too much too soon" (TMTS.) You will also reach various "break-through" points where everything seems to come together. Your form will finally click and everything will feel great. You will be tempted to try out your newly-perfected form. It will once again be important to exercise caution. Do not increase your mileage more than 10-15% per week or pace by more than 15 seconds per mile per week. By being cautious, your transition to barefoot running should be smooth and injury-free!

For regular, long-term shod runners, a big challenge is drastically dialing back the miles upon flipping to barefoot. A common strategy is to keep going with shoes in parallel and wean over to barefoot miles with time. However once you get going, you probably won't feel like putting shoes back on. My advice is to embrace the chance to start over. It is the nature of the beast to plateau over time in any endeavor. Celebrate the opportunity to re-experience rapid change and progress. It's exciting to double your mileage in the first week or two (albeit only from half mile runs up to full mile). Enjoy the sore calves and the re-strengthening of your neglected foot muscles. Savor the challenge of stretching shortened tendons. And, take the opportunity to augment your caloric burn with some cross training; yoga, for example, is wonderful in bare feet.

Phillip Odence
http://odence.wordpress.com/

Concept—Running Happy

"Fitness has to be fun. If it is not play, there will be no fitness. Play, you see, is the process. Fitness is merely the product."
—George Sheehan

 All too often, I see other runners with either a scowl or apparently wincing in pain. It is abundantly clear they are not enjoying themselves. Running should be enjoyable, especially when we ditch the shoes! Before you begin your journey into barefoot or minimalist shoe running, always keep the following ideas in mind:

- *Smile often.* First, it makes others smile. It is wonderful publicity for barefoot running. Second, barefoot running is enjoyable! It's like being a kid again. Embrace your inner-child! Third, by smiling, you are providing feedback to your brain that actually makes you feel happier (Kleinke, et. al., 1998) thus making the activity more fun!

- *Be nice.* If you encounter another runner, say "Hi." Other people mirror our behaviors. If half of the runners on the road and trails were friendly and nice, they would convert the other "grumpy" half.

- *Thank volunteers at races.* They are taking valuable time out of their day to help YOU. Do not complain, scold, or belittle them. If they do not fill your water bottle to your satisfaction, thank them and do it yourself next time. If you follow the first two rules, this one should take care of itself.

Issue—Minimalist Shoe or Barefoot?

 It is common for new barefoot runners to have a desire to "ease into" barefoot running by using a minimalist shoe (Vibram FiveFingers®, Terra Plana's EVO®, Feelmax® shoes, cross country racing flats, huarache sandals, etc). I have found it is better to learn the proper form of barefoot running first, and then use minimalist shoes as needed.

If you begin by wearing minimalist shoes, you may be insulating your best form of feedback—the soles of your feet. Learning to run barefoot first generally speeds the transition. Good form combined with properly strengthening your feet faster allow a barefoot runner to reach his or her goals faster.

To learn good form using my methods, it is critical that your brain receive accurate sensory feedback from the rest of your body. This is especially true of your feet. The soles of your feet will tell you if you are over-striding, running too fast, or creating too much friction. If you cover your feet even with a minimalist shoe such as the Vibrams, you will short-circuit that neural pathway.

Shoes have one more distinct disadvantage. The more we place between the soles of our feet and the ground, the more force we generate when our foot touches the ground.

Activity—Spend Time Barefoot

Spending your days barefoot is an excellent way to begin training your brain and the rest of your body. At home I rarely wear shoes, even in the winter. Outdoors, as well, I try to be barefoot as much as possible.

If your house contains a variety of different surfaces, this will help teach your brain to discriminate between small variations under foot. When moving around your house, pay close attention to the feeling of the different surfaces. Being aware of the tactile sensations being felt by your foot is critically important as you begin more rigorous activities.

My fellow Society for Barefoot Living (www.barefooters.org) members try to spend the vast majority of their time barefoot. This group advocates for the acceptance of a barefoot lifestyle by challenging business policies. Most people assume there are health department regulations that require shoes to be worn in businesses. Actually, there are no states that have such laws. A handful of municipalities have such laws, but they are very rare. It is also perfectly legal to drive barefoot (check your local laws in case of exceptions).

Concept—"Toughening" the Soles of Your Feet

The idea of "toughening" the soles of your feet is one of the most misunderstood concepts in barefoot running. There is no need to do anything special to your feet. Some newer barefoot runners have tried some strange methods to speed the process of "toughening" their soles including rubbing their feet with sand paper or dunking them in ice water.

If you begin slowly and follow my plan, your feet will adapt. Specifically, your skin will become more resilient to friction. Contrary to popular belief, you do not develop hard calluses on your soles. The skin becomes very smooth, much like soft leather. In my opinion, the more important adaptation has to

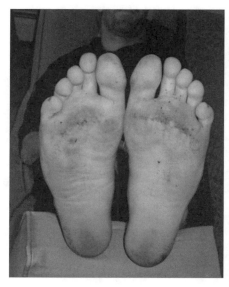

do with tactile recognition. Through practice and experience, your soles will develop the ability to "feel" the terrain under foot—a major element in preventing injury. It is also important that you be cautious and keep from doing too much too soon.

Once you become more experienced, the increased tactile sensation will allow your feet to immediately react in the event you step on something sharp and/or painful. After years of barefoot running, I have developed the ability to run on leaf or snow covered trails through my ability to "feel" the hidden terrain. With practice and experience, you can develop this skill, too!

Jesse Scott, a friend and fellow barefoot/minimalist shoe ultrarunner, described this process as your foot "melts" over the obstacle. This "melting" results from the reflexive relaxing of the foot when nerves detect something painful.

Activity—Barefoot Walking

 One of the best methods to prepare for barefoot running is spending time walking barefoot. Quite literally, you have to learn to walk before you run. Walking barefoot will reduce the likelihood of injury once you begin running.

When walking barefoot, there is some disagreement on form. Some barefoot practitioners will recommend using a midfoot strike; others will recommend a heel strike. Either will work as long as it is comfortable.

If comfortable, it is advantageous to use a midfoot strike while taking shorter, more frequent steps (higher cadence, shorter stride length). This will help strengthen your feet and acclimate you to good barefoot running form.

Barefoot walking will also help condition your soles for barefoot running. As mentioned in the previous section, the soles of your feet do not develop calluses. Instead, your feet develop smooth, tough skin.

When beginning to navigate your environment barefoot, your feet will be very sensitive to everything. It is similar to going from a dark room to a lit room—as your eyes experience a short period of adjustment. For those in colder climates, you may experience the same sensation when you start going barefoot for the first time each season after winter though you will quickly adapt to the sensations. New barefoot runners are often preoccupied with this sensitivity. Rest assured, you will quickly adapt to this new feeling.

It is important to remember to look where you are walking by developing the habit of quickly scanning the terrain you are about to walk over. This skill will be critical once you begin running.

As you learn to run with ease and efficiency, you will begin exploring new terrain. Taking time to walk over new terrain prior to running will help build the skills and adaptations that are necessary. Remember, walk before running.

Barefoot walking can be good practice to adapt a run/walk strategy for races. This strategy is often used by newer runners to help cover a distance that would otherwise be difficult to achieve through running alone. It is also a common strategy for running ultramarathons. If you have aspirations to run those distances, learning to walk barefoot now will pay dividends in the future.

Concept—Relax Like a Wet Noodle

 Relaxation is one of the fundamental skills all barefoot runners share and is critical to developing the ability to run with little impact. You cannot run softly if you are tense. Like all physical activity, running itself has some degree of tension. Exercise, as with all running, causes the sympathetic nervous system to activate, which increases heart rate, blood pressure, and all the other elements of the human "fight or flight" response system. When the body is preparing for physical activity; relaxation is difficult. However, like every other element of barefoot running, this response can be managed with enough practice.

I find it helpful to use visualization to relax my arms and legs which I pretend loose and free-flowing, like wet noodles. Then I actually move them around as if they are stands of cooked spaghetti. Odd? Perhaps. But it really does help. Try it yourself next time you are walking or running, imagine your arms and legs are loose and free—like wet noodles.

In the next section, I will give you a very basic exercise to help put that visualization to practice in order to help you to achieve a greater level of relaxation.

Activity—Deep Breathing for Relaxation

 Deep breathing is a very basic method for forcing your body's sympathetic nervous system to deactivate and make the "wet noodle" visualization even easier to accomplish.

Find a quiet spot where you can comfortably sit or lie down. The process is easy. I do this by inhaling slowly while I count to five, then exhaling for the same count. Repeat for two or three minutes.

You will notice an immediate difference as the tension leaves your body. Your arms and legs will start to feel heavier as your heart rate slows down. For me the imagery at this point is of the tension flowing down my body to my arms and legs, and flowing out of my fingers and toes.

After a few minutes, slowly open your eyes. Your entire body should feel more relaxed. At this point, you should be able to continue any activities while remaining very relaxed.

The deep breathing will help augment the "wet noodle" visualization by activating the underlying physiological process responsible for relaxation. It is also useful for those with small children—especially if they are as "spirited" as mine!

Concept—Lift Feet

 Beyond relaxation another skill that is nearly universal is lifting your feet. Most shod runners will use a heel strike where the heel hits the ground first in front of the body's center of gravity (over-striding.)

This causes two problems. First, it acts as a slight braking action that interferes with your forward progress and wastes a tremendous amount of energy with every step. Second, it causes undue stress on your entire body because of the force of the strike.

This force is thought to be a major contributor to the many pains traditional shod runners experience. The solution is to allow your feet to softly touch the ground under your center of gravity. The easiest way to achieve this is to focus on lifting your foot off the ground instead of driving it into the ground. I like to imagine I'm running on hot coals. The imagery helps me focus on keeping my feet from burning by lifting naturally.

Runners can accomplish this lifting motion in various ways using different muscle groups. I believe the exact method is inconsequential. The important point is that you are lifting which automatically results in a softer step. If we focus on lifting, we forget about the other foot that is touching the ground which automatically causes the foot to land with less force.

The focus on lifting the feet will also help prevent another common problem among new barefoot runners: "pushing off." Many runners mistakenly believe their forward motion is created by using the foot on the ground as an anchor point and pushing off against that anchor to generate forward motion.

This "pushing off" technique causes undue stress on the body, especially the legs and feet. It also causes runners to land with much more force than they would if they focused on lifting their feet. In future sections, I will discuss the safer, more efficient method of using the foot-lift to propel you forward.

Concept—Foot-Kiss

 In addition to the foot-lift, there is the foot-kiss, traditionally known as the foot "strike," which implies that it is a violent collision between your foot and the ground. It is actually the exact opposite. Your foot should gently touch the ground with as little force as possible as if your foot is gently "kissing" the ground.

Many barefoot runners will debate the exact method you should use as your foot touches the ground. Should you land on the ball of your foot, on your forefoot, or the heel first? After observing many barefoot runners, I have concluded that it does not really matter which part of your foot touches the ground first.

There are two important points. First, your foot must gently kiss (or touch) the ground, like a gentle peck on the cheek. Second, no matter which part touches first, the rest of your foot must follow by quickly touching. The desired result is that your entire foot will be momentarily be in contact with the ground.

In the next session, the walk in place drill, you will begin to develop a feel for the part of your foot that is most comfortable touching first. If you need a place to begin, I suggest starting with a midfoot kiss which appears to be the most common technique. If you find something to be more comfortable, use it—since the key to developing good form is listening to your body.

Activity—Walk in Place Drill

Once comfortable with lifting foot and foot-kiss concepts, it is time to combine them into the walk in place drill. The purpose of this drill is twofold. First, it will help strengthen your anatomy in preparation for running. Second, it will teach you the very basic elements of proper form. The movements you perform in this drill will translate directly to actual walking and running.

Start by relaxing using the deep breathing exercise if necessary. Next, stand on a hard smooth surface. Your posture should be upright with your arms and legs relaxed. Practice lifting one foot while your other foot is a few inches off the ground. Next, immediately shift your focus to lifting your other foot. You will automatically lower the first foot and softly kiss the ground.

Focusing on raising the other foot is the key to success. Your brain will automatically allow the first foot to touch the ground using what should be an ideal foot touch. Going slowly at first, alternate this lifting between feet. If you find you are paying too much attention to the foot touching the ground, stop for a moment until you are able shift your to concentration to lifting.

The goal is to try to make as little noise as possible by acclimating your body to the muscle movements needed to walk and run softly. Practiced often, your brain will begin to develop the muscle memory needed to repeat this movement.

This drill can be practiced multiple times per day for varying amounts of time. You can practice it almost anywhere; at home when cooking dinner, in the elevator at work, even in airplane restrooms! If you find your form or concentration slipping, stop and take a break. It is best done in short bursts, slowly increasing over time. I would recommend starting with one minute then increasing one minute per day until you reach five minutes. Once you can do this without any pain or discomfort, you are ready to move to the next stage.

Activity—Jump Drill

The jump drill is designed as a strengthening exercise. Find a hard, smooth surface. Stand with your feet shoulder-width apart. Keep your upper body and back perpendicular to the ground. Bend at your knees until your knees reach about a 90° angle. Now jump up off the ground in one quick, smooth motion. When you land, you will want to use your feet, ankles, and knees to absorb as much of the impact as possible. You should try to land as quietly as possible.

When doing the jump drill, I like to imagine I am a cat jumping off a chair. Cats always seem to land without sound, so the analogy works for me. Repeat this five times in a row, several times per day. Like the walk in place drill, the jump drill can be done throughout all stages to help strengthen your feet, ankles, knees, legs, and hips.

Activity—Marble Drill

This is the final pre-running drill. Barefoot running requires the use of many muscles that rarely get used when running in traditional running shoes. Walking in place and the jump drill will help develop strength, but the marble drill will help with other muscle groups that are rarely used but critical while running barefoot.

The drill is best done with the support of a chair and can be done standing or sitting. It requires you to spread small objects around on the floor. Any small objects will work including building blocks, marbles, small rocks, or dice. After spreading the objects around on the floor, practice picking them up with your toes by curling them around the object. Move the object a few inches to one side, and then drop it on the floor.

At the end of one minute, alternate feet. Increase the workout by one minute per day for the duration of this stage.

The marble drill will help strengthen the musculature of your feet. If you have small children and/or a lot of small toys, try using your toes to pick up the toys. My messy children have done wonders for my own foot strength!

Tips on Proper Forefoot or Midfoot Strike Form

There is no single "perfect running form." Everyone's body is different and no single technique could be best for everyone. Here are some general tips:

A good landing should feel gentle, relaxed and compliant. You typically land on the ball of your foot towards the lateral side. After the front of your foot lands, let the heel down gradually, bringing the foot and lower leg to a gentle landing as you dorsiflex your ankle under the control of your calf muscles. It's like when you land from a jump, flexing the hip, knee and ankle. Again, the landing should feel soft, springy, and comfortable. It's probably good to land with the foot nearly horizontal so you don't have to work the calves too much.

Do not over stride (land with your foot too far in front of your hips). Over striding while forefoot or midfoot striking requires you to point your toe more than necessary, adding stress to the calf muscles, Achilles tendon, and the arch of the foot. It often feels as if your feet are striking the ground beneath your hips. In this respect it feels like "running in place" (as runners sometimes do when waiting to cross a street). It is also similar to the way one's feet land when skipping rope.

A good way to tell if you are landing properly is to run totally barefoot on a hard, smooth surface (e.g. pavement) that is free of debris. Sensory feedback will quickly tell you if you are landing too hard. If you run barefoot on too soft a surface like a beach, you might not learn proper form.

Daniel Lieberman, PhD., et. al.
Reprinted with permission from:
http://www.barefootrunning.fas.harvard.edu
© 2010 Daniel Lieberman. All rights reserved.

Starting to Run Barefoot
Taking your first strides

While the previous section laid the groundwork, the purpose of this stage is to actually begin barefoot running. You have worked on developing strength, tactile sensations, and the basic elements of barefoot running form. During this stage, you put the "foot-lift" and "foot-kiss" elements together to start developing your own unique barefoot running form.

By the end of this stage, you will have developed the ability to run barefoot! In subsequent stages, you will use that perfect form to advance both speed and distance to help reach your running goals.

You will have successfully completed this stage when:

- You are able to run one and a half miles without pain during or after the run,
- You feel comfortable running in a relaxed, smooth manner with a cadence of at least 180 steps per minute.

Activity—Progressive Relaxation

 In the previous stage, I described the use of deep breathing to facilitate relaxation. During this stage, we add another technique known as progressive relaxation which is a technique I used with great success while coaching football. At that time I used it to help placekickers relax prior to kicking field goals and extra points. Like deep breathing, this method will help turn off your "fight or flight" response since relaxation is a critical barefoot running skill.

Progressive relaxation involves tensing various muscle groups, holding it for five seconds, and then slowly relaxing. Using this technique, cycle through all of the major muscle groups. The repeated release of tension activates your parasympathetic nervous system and deactivates your sympathetic system.

When I use progressive relaxation, I use the following order of muscle groups: feet, calves, thighs, hips, buttocks, abdominal muscles, lower back, chest, upper back and shoulders, upper arms, forearms, hands, neck, and face. You can determine your own order of progression.

For added effectiveness, I do a few minutes of deep breathing before starting progressive relaxation. Once finished, your body should be in the ideal relaxed state to begin barefoot running.

Concept—Cadence/Stride

 A fundamental difference between barefoot or minimalist shoe running and traditional cushioned running shoes, is the rate at which your feet touch the ground. Most runners that wear traditional running shoes will strike the ground approximately 140–160 times per minute. Barefoot and minimalist shoe runners will touch the ground at a significantly higher rate. The minimum cadence a barefoot runner should use is around 180 steps per minute. I use an even higher cadence averaging approximately 200 steps per minute.

This faster cadence causes two significant changes to your running form. First, it shortens your stride which helps prevent over-striding where your foot touches the ground in front of your body.

Second, it helps develop a more efficient form by limiting excessive movement resulting in a shorter stride with less vertical movement.

Though the barefoot running stride is shorter, the exact length will be determined by the runners own unique physical characteristics. The idea is to find a cadence greater than about 180 steps per minute coupled with a relatively short stride length that results in the greatest comfort.

Some barefoot runners will find their cadence slower than 180 steps per minute, which is acceptable; especially if running slowly. Again, the goal is to prevent overstriding.

Activity—Metronome Drill

The tool required for this drill is a metronome. One can be found at: http://www. reztronics.com/prod01.htm. If the files are not available, Google "metronome." If you prefer music, "Turning Japanese" by The Vapors (thanks to PeaceKaren from the *Runners World* Barefoot Running Forum) has 180 beats per minute.

The metronome drill will teach you the ideal cadence for barefoot running. Download the "180" file. Play it on your computer or MP3 player. Most people use a metronome by timing the beats to each foot strike. I prefer to lift my foot with each beat because it creates a subtle psychological effect of lightening each foot touch. Scott Schnieder gave me this tip: it is easiest to combine this drill with the slow running drill introduced later in this stage.

Some people may have a difficult time keeping up with the beat. I fall in this category. I found it to be as effective to simply count the number of times I lift my foot for a 30 second period, then multiply that by two. If my cadence is below 180, I take smaller, faster steps.

Concept—Fall Forward and Keep Feet Under Body

 The idea of running with your feet kissing the ground directly under your center of gravity is one of the fundamental elements all barefoot runners share. In contrast, many shod runners will touch the ground in front of their center of gravity as I explained earlier. It is far more efficient to move that point of contact back so your feet come in contact with the ground under you. For most people, this process automatically occurs when they shorten their stride, increase cadence, and use more of a midfoot touch.

Some people will still struggle with this concept. An easy way to implement it is to use a slight forward lean, which many barefoot runners use though it is not necessarily universal. Personally, I do not use much of a lean most of the time, but many find it useful. The idea is to keep your midsection (core) tense and lean slightly forward at the ankles.

To visualize what this looks like, I think of a ski jumper. They keep their entire body rigid but lean out over their skis by bending at the ankles. The barefoot running lean isn't nearly as pronounced, but that should give you the general idea. When done while running, it will give a slight sensation like you are falling forward. If you combine this with lifting your feet, you will achieve forward motion. In the next section, I will present a drill that will help you learn the forward lean.

Activity—Wall Drill

The wall drill is designed to help you understand the feeling of leaning forward while running. This drill can be used to help develop the feel for leaning at the ankles. Stand upright about six inches from a wall. Keeping your body straight, lean forward by bending at the ankles until your forehead touches the wall.

Again, visualize a ski jumper as they fly through the air. How you feel when leaning on the wall is the approximate forward lean you should have when barefoot running. This helps contribute to the "falling forward" feeling I described in the last section.

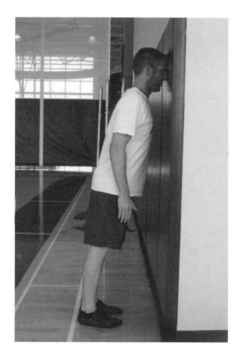

Concept—Posture (Head, Torso, Arms, and Knees)

 The basic elements of barefoot running have already been discussed. The remaining parts of your body are important but not as universal as those previously mentioned. When starting barefoot running, I would recommend the following:

- *Head*—Level with eyes scanning the ground. See the note below about scanning the terrain you are traversing.
- *Midsection*—You do not want to slouch. While it is important for your arms and legs to be very loose, your midsection and torso should be rigid.
- *Arms*—Elbows should be bent with arms held close to the body. Do not allow your arms to swing across your body.
- *Knees*—Should be bent slightly throughout your stride. At no time should your knees be fully extended. Likewise, do not bend them excessively.

When running barefoot, you have little or no protection against glass, nails, thorns, or other such debris to avoid potential dangers. It is absolutely critical to develop your skill at analyzing the terrain immediately in front of you.

With practice, this skill will become automatic. Until that occurs, ALWAYS watch your path. If you encounter an area that contains hazards, it is best to avoid that area.

One final area of concern is tripping or stubbing your toes on objects. My only two barefoot injuries came about because of this. Once I tripped on a root when running a 50-miler while checking my watch. The other time I tripped on a speed bump while on a training run because I was looking at a clock tower. In both cases, my falls could have been prevented, had I not been distracted.

Again, it is critically important to watch your path to identify potential hazards and to pick your feet up high enough to avoid tripping over hazards.

Feel the Ground Beneath Your Feet

You have never truly experienced running until you have gone on a barefoot run and felt the ground beneath your feet. The tens of thousands of nerve endings in your feet provide an experience which will transcend your previous runner's high.

Every runner should run barefoot to learn their fundamentals and build strong, healthy feet. Once a strong foundation has been established then, and only then, a decision can be made of barefoot or shod for running.

I witnessed Jason hit his low during a 100 mile run ... and push through to successfully finish. He doesn't just write about this stuff ... he does it himself.

Barefoot running can be an odd, slow, painful experience ... but it does not have to be! Follow Jason's advice to avoid the mistakes and pitfalls many barefoot runners run into.

Michael Helton
Minimalist shoe expert and pacer extraordinaire

When you begin barefoot running, smooth, hard terrain is ideal. Smooth asphalt roads, concrete sidewalks, smooth running tracks, or gymnasium floors are good options. Any choice should be free of debris. A smooth, hard surface will serve two purposes: First, the hardness will give better feedback than soft surfaces by forcing you to run gently. Second, it will reinforce the "foot-kiss" concept. The smoothness of the surface will prevent unnecessary friction in the beginning stages of learning. It is possible to learn on a rough surface, but I've found it to be distracting.

Once you develop a feel for form and have some degree of success (run a mile or two barefoot without pain during or after the run), you can graduate to different surfaces.

It is advised to avoid soft, forgiving surfaces like grass or sand. Running barefoot on a surface such as grass may be tempting because it feels good, but the softness can inhibit your brain's ability to provide good feedback. Soft ground acts much like the thick, cushioned padding of traditional running shoes. It can hide bad form resulting in a longer learning period.

Once you learn good form, running on grass and sand is perfectly acceptable. Running over sand dunes along Lake Michigan is one of my favorite workouts.

Activity—Run/Walk Drill

 The run/walk drill is a good precursor to beginning barefoot running. Its purpose is to make a transition between walking in place, walking barefoot, and running barefoot. To begin, find a smooth, hard surface that will allow you to run a moderate distance.

Start by walking relaxed in place for 30 seconds followed by moving in a slow walk forward for another 30 seconds. The key is to maintain the same relaxed foot lift and gentle touch you practiced in the previous drills. Upon completing the 30 seconds of walking, move to a slow run. The key to the run portion is to maintain the relaxed foot-lift, gentle touch, and 180 step cadence for the entire 30 seconds.

After the time expires, slow down to a walking pace as you did before the run. After 30 seconds, stop and walk in place. Repeat this cycle three times. On subsequent days, add one cycle to each practice session to increase the amount of time doing the drill. This drill will help you put each element together into one complete package.

Once you can successfully make the transition between walking in place, slow walking, and slow running, you will be ready to move on to the next activity: slow running.

Activity—Slow Running

Slow running is the pinnacle activity of the second stage. After you spend some time strengthening your body, and you develop some of the basic barefoot running skills, you will be ready to start running. By this time you will have developed an excellent foundation to make the transition to barefoot running.

To begin, find a smooth, hard surface free of debris. Do the deep breathing drill or progressive relaxation drill to assure you are in a relaxed state. Start by slowly walking in place by focusing on lifting your feet. After a few steps, start moving forward into a slow walk. Gradually increase your cadence until

71

you reach the 180 mark. You should now be running at a slow pace. Continue to stay as relaxed as possible. Focus on lifting one foot while the other foot is gently kissing the ground.

Depending on your experience level, limit your first run to ¼ to ½ mile. If you feel any pain, stop. After each "run" day, schedule a rest day. This will allow your body to always have the opportunity to heal. Remember, you are using muscles, tendons, ligaments, and bones that have not had to work for years!

During your rest day assess any potential soft-tissue damage that may have occurred. Soft tissue damage does not always appear immediately after a workout. Each subsequent "run" day, you can increase the mileage by ⅛ to ¼ miles. Once you reach 1-½ to 2 miles, you should be ready to advance to the next stage.

Concept—Run Like a Ninja

 Once you master that skill of running relaxed, it is time to add another element that was briefly discussed earlier: running softly or running light.

To begin, make sure you are in an area free of obstacles, debris, or walls. Close your eyes and run for about 25 to 50 yards.

Listen carefully to the sounds your feet are making as they touch the ground. Ideally, they should make little or no noise. If you hear significant noise, your feet are not softly "kissing" the ground. Refine your form until you can run silently while slowing your running pace.

To help achieve this concept, I like to imagine one of two scenarios. First, I will pretend I am a ninja silently sneaking around my environment.

If you are not familiar with ninjas, I recommend using another analogy such as a cat stalking prey.

Using analogies like this serve two purposes: They add an element of fun to training and help distract our conscious mind so we don't "over-think" running. It is an easy way to allow your brain to receive, interpret, and react to the information coming in from your soles and the rest of your body.

Issue—Blisters

Blisters are a fairly common issue for the new barefoot runner and result from a combination of heat, friction, and moisture. If all three are present, blisters tend to form quickly.

Friction is usually the main culprit with moisture being a non-issue unless you are running in mud or rain. Heat can be an issue if running on a hot surface such as asphalt on a sunny day or some treadmills.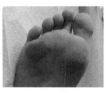

If blisters do develop, they can be an indicator that your form is not quite as good as it could be. Where blisters develop can be very informative. When blisters develop on the heel, that is usually an indicator that you are heel striking or over-striding. If they develop on the toes or the ball of the foot at the base of your toes, that can be an indicator that you are "pushing off" with each stride. Blisters that form along the outer edge of the sole of your foot usually indicate that your foot is not landing under your center of gravity. If you do develop blisters, slow down. You are most likely running too fast or too long for your current skill level.

As for treating blisters, it is recommended that you do not pop them. That will increase the likelihood of infection. After some time, on their own, the blister may pop and eventually reveal soft, sensitive skin. Be very careful with this new skin; it is not yet acclimated to the rigors of barefoot running.

When I develop blisters it usually involves running too fast for my current level of acclimation. Once the blisters pop and the old skin tears away (or I remove it), I cover the area with extra-adhesive bandages. I may have to do this for a week or two while waiting for new skin to grow. To facilitate this process, I will walk around barefoot once the wounds are adequately healed.

Issue—Handling Overly Technical Advice

Sometimes new barefoot runners will solicit advice from more experienced barefoot runners. While the sharing of information is always a good thing, sometimes the new barefoot runner can be overloaded with information.

Be aware each new barefoot runner must learn to listen to their own body. For example, if a runner concentrates on keeping their knees bent at a precise angle, their brain can become too distracted to respond to the input being received from their body. It is best to hold off on soliciting advice on specific details. Once you get a feel for your ideal form, then you will be free to tinker with the small details. Remember, barefoot running is about feeling, not thinking.

In the event you follow the advice in this book, practice the drills, put in the time, and are still experiencing difficulty, one of the previously-mentioned running programs may be of benefit.

In my experience, about 10–15% of people that start barefoot running using these methods will have considerable difficulty. Some people have great difficulty interpreting the feedback their body provides.

Intermediate Barefoot Running
Now the fun really begins!

The intermediate stage introduces you to activities and concepts that will help you advance as a barefoot runner. Before beginning this stage, you should be able to run 1-½ miles barefoot without pain during or after the run in a relaxed, light form. This section introduces a variety of challenges that will help hone your skills as a barefoot runner and include adding hills and varied terrain to your training. It also introduces guidelines to begin expanding both speed (pace) and distance.

Concept—Run Efficiently

 The next concept to master is the ability to run efficiently. At this stage you should be adept at running with a relaxed, smooth form. Now is the time to systematically eliminate all wasted movement to gracefully "float" over the ground.

Being able to run smooth is the last concept prior to increasing speed and distance. To run efficiently, you must be both relaxed and be able to run by gently touching the ground with each step.

To add efficiency, make sure all body parts are moving forward. Don't allow your arms or legs to swing wildly from side-to-side. Flailing is a tell-tale sign of inefficiency. Only lift your feet as high as necessary to clear the tallest obstacles in your path. Work on limiting your vertical up-and-down movement as much as possible.

Some runners will waste energy and increase shock by "hopping" with every step. In almost every case, hopping is caused by overstriding.

One analogy I've found useful is imagining I am a graceful animal, such as a gazelle. Other times, I may think I am water smoothly flowing over the terrain.

Concept—Experimentation

*"Each of us is an experiment of one—observer and subject—
making choices, living with them, recording the effects."*
—George Sheehan

Learning to run barefoot will require you to try
many different techniques and methods. To be
successful you must be open to experimentation;
adopting anything that works and discarding
anything that does not.

Whenever you encounter something new, try it a few times.
If it seems to lead to improvement, stick with it. If not, revert
back to what worked best. When going through this process,
it is important to change only one variable at a time. If you
attempt to change multiple things, it will be impossible to
determine which variables were successful or unsuccessful.
Some find it helpful to keep a journal of the changes they try
to determine what does and does not work.

Studying other running techniques like Good Form
Running®, Evolution Running®, ChiRunning®, and Pose® can
be useful in this regard. Each method will have many different
teaching points and drills that can be used for experimentation.

Activity—Fartlek Run

A Fartlek run is a training run of varying speed with
no predetermined pace. You run based on feel. When
doing Fartlek runs, start slow to warm up. Once
warm, speed up to the fastest pace you are currently
comfortable running. This will be determined by your barefoot
experience. If you are new to barefoot running, this will be a
slow pace. After several months of barefoot running, this pace
will approach or even surpass your 5K pace.

For myself I will run at this pace for a short time, perhaps
one minute. I do not predetermine the time, I just run based
on feel. Once I tire, I will slow down to a near-walking

pace. Sometimes I will actually walk. Once I am sufficiently recovered, I will speed up again. The total time I spend on this run will usually be predetermined, but the actual content of the run will be based on how I feel during the run. This activity can be completed once or twice per week.

Fartlek runs constitute a major component of my training (see appendix).

Issue—Top Of the Foot Pain (TOFP)

 One of the dangers of beginning barefoot running is doing too much too soon. Your feet have likely spent most of their active life confined in shoes. Shoes weaken the bones, muscles, ligaments, and tendons of your feet. The skin on the soles of your feet will not be accustomed to the sensory input from the ground. In order to prevent injuries, it is important to begin barefoot running cautiously.

Do not give in to the temptation to "run through the pain." The soft-tissue injuries that can occur during the foot-strengthening process can set your progress back by weeks or even months. TOO MUCH TOO SOON injuries are the greatest obstacle to successfully transitioning to barefoot running!

One fairly universal complaint is often referred to as the "top of the foot pain," or metatarsalgia. It feels like a dull ache on the top side of your foot. This seems to be a function of your foot anatomy adapting to the different stresses of using new muscles, tendons, and ligaments. Mild soreness is not a major issue and generally you can train through this dull ache. If the pain becomes moderate to severe, stop. Rest until the pain subsides. Give this process time, and the rewards will be great!

Because barefoot running feels wonderful it is important to follow a conservative plan even if your feet feel great in the beginning. Going too fast may result in a myriad of injuries, including tendon and ligament damage, excessive blisters, stress fractures, and other over-use type injuries. If at any time you experience pain, STOP! Add a second day of rest, and then try again. Continue until you are pain-free. In the event you experience severe pain, medical treatment should be sought.

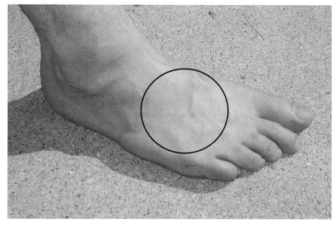

Common "top of the foot pain" location

Issue—Achilles/Calf Pain

 Aside from TOFP, the other common issue experienced by new barefoot or minimalist shoe runners is calf and/or Achilles pain or tightness. The cause of this is obvious. Traditional shoes, running or otherwise, have a built-up heel that is higher than the forefoot region of the shoe. Think of high heels, just not quite so dramatic. The more we wear these shoes, the more we chronically shorten the Achilles tendon.

When we move to barefoot or minimalist shoe activities, the Achilles tendon is stretched. This stretching causes calf tightness. If we are not patient in the transition to barefoot or minimalist shoes, we run the risk of injuring this area. Also, the tightness of the calf and Achilles tendon can lead to other problems such as plantar fasciitis.

Some degree of tightness or soreness of the calf muscle is expected and is the normal consequence of using a muscle that has been allowed to weaken for years. If you are patient, there is no danger. However, if you fall victim to doing too much too soon, it is possible to develop a litany of problems associated with the calf muscles and Achilles tendon. If you experience any acute or moderate pain, stop immediately and seek medical treatment. Rest until the pain subsides, then ease back into your training schedule.

Issue—Shin Splints

 Shin splints are a fairly common ailment in shod runners, but rare among barefoot runners. It is believed to be caused by combining a heel strike with overstriding. When the heel hits the ground, the force drives the forefoot down in a plantarflexion position. This rapid, pounding stress causes the shin muscles to stretch, which causes an involuntary contraction and is believed to be the cause of the pain.

If you experience shin splints when running barefoot, it is almost always caused by overstriding. This is easy to correct. Simply focus on your feet touching the ground under your center of gravity, not in front. I've found the easiest way to accomplish this is to shorten your stride and increase your cadence.

Activity—Hills

Running on hills present a new challenge as they often require at least some modification of form. If you have aspirations of trail running, learning to effectively navigate hills will be a necessity. The key to effective hill running is not much different than learning to run on any other surface or terrain. Start slow and gradually develop speed.

Hill running technique tends to be a hotly-debated topic for barefoot runners with individual runners having their own opinion on the best technique for tackling hills. Generally, I recommend using the same form for going up hills as when running on flat roads or sidewalks. To reduce the likelihood of injury, it may be helpful to increase your cadence and decrease your stride length. Also, if running on trails, some prefer to power-hike up the hill.

I have found uphill running to be easier when running barefoot. As Barefoot Ted has accurately pointed out, the bare foot acts as a traction-control system allowing you to immediately feel any slippage under foot. With practice, you can adjust your weight and use your toes to grip the ground resulting in a dramatic increase in efficiency.

Downhill on trails can be a little more difficult depending on the terrain. The fundamental problem lies in the midfoot landing used by most barefoot runners. If you land on your forefoot, your foot will be in a plantarflexion position (foot pointing down) which can put added stress on your knees.

Shod runners avoid this by landing on their heels as they descend. Barefoot runners can do this, but the shock of landing on the heel can lead to injury.

A better solution is to use what I call the "zig-zag" run. If you have even watched downhill or mogul skiers, the technique will seem familiar. Start the descent by pointing your toes to the left at a 45° angle to the base of the hill. Take a few quick, short steps; turn 90° to the right ending up facing the right at a 45° angle to the base of the hill. Take a few steps, and then repeat the process.

This technique will disperse the workload among different muscles and reduce the likelihood of injuring tendons and ligament.

Tips on Transitioning to Forefoot or Midfoot Striking

Forefoot striking barefoot or in minimal footwear requires you to use muscles in your feet (mostly in the arch) that are probably very weak. Running this way also requires much more strength in your calf muscles than heel striking because these muscles must contract eccentrically (while lengthening) to ease the heel onto the ground following the landing. Novice forefoot and midfoot strikers typically experience tired feet, and very stiff, sore calf muscles. In addition, the Achilles tendon often gets very stiff. This is normal and eventually goes away, but you can do several things to ease the transition:

Build up slowly! If you vigorously work out any weak muscles in your body, they will become sore and stiff. Your foot and calf muscles are no exception. So please, don't overdo it because you will probably injure yourself if you do too much too soon.

Start by frequently walking around barefoot.

First week: no more than a quarter mile to one mile every other day.

Increase your distance by no more than 10% per week. This is not a hard and fast rule, but a general guide. If your muscles remain sore, do not increase your training. Take an extra day off or maintain your distance for another week.

Stop and let your body heal if you experience pain. Sore, tired muscles are normal, but bone, joint, or soft-tissue pain are signs of injury.

Be patient and build gradually. It takes months to make the transition.

If you are currently running a lot, you don't need to drastically reduce your mileage. Instead, supplement forefoot or midfoot striking with running the way you ran before beginning the transition. Over the course of several months, gradually increase the proportion of forefoot or midfoot striking and reduce the proportion of running in your old style. Use the same 10% per week guideline in increasing the amount of running you do forefoot striking.

It is essential to stretch your calves and hamstrings carefully and regularly as you make the transition. To break down scar tissue, frequently massage your calf muscles and arches. This will help your muscles to heal and get stronger.

Listen to your feet. Stop if your arches are hurting, if the top of your foot is hurting, or if anything else hurts! Sometimes arch and foot pain occurs from landing with your feet too far forward relative to your hips and having to point your toes too much. It can also occur from landing with too rigid a foot and not letting your heel drop gently.

Many people who run very slowly find that forefoot striking actually makes them run a little faster.

Daniel Lieberman, PhD., et. al.
Reprinted with permission from:
http://www.barefootrunning.fas.harvard.edu

Concept—Varied Terrain

 It is possible to run on any terrain barefoot with practice. I advocate starting on a smooth, hard surface such as asphalt or concrete, and then slowly add an ever-increasing variety of progressively more difficult terrain. This ever-increasing challenge will help hone your skills as a barefoot runner. While it is very tempting to start on very soft, forgiving terrain (such as grass), this greatly limits the feedback your feet receive. The result may be that poor form may go unnoticed. Ken Bob Saxton (therunningbarefoot. org) describes running on grass as "dessert:" something that should be enjoyed after learning to run on harder terrain.

As for terrain, it is ALWAYS important to watch the ground on which you run. The distance upon which you fix your gaze is dependent on the ruggedness of the terrain. Smooth asphalt with little or no debris will allow you to watch the ground 50 feet in front of you and still be able to avoid obstacles. Very

technical trails with lots of rugged rocks, roots, and other such debris will require you to watch only a few feet in front of you.

In either case, you eventually develop foot-eye coordination as your eyes scan the terrain ahead. Your brain will create a cognitive map of that terrain then automatically guide your feet to the areas that are free of debris. It is a skill that is easily practiced.

On smooth, clear asphalt, you can practice this skill by avoiding small cracks, paint marks, or any other "obstacle." Eventually, you can advance to areas that may have more challenging obstacles. The key is to move at a slow pace in the beginning. Walking first on moderately difficult terrain is another excellent training tool.

Another handy skill that develops is the ability to immediately react in the event you step on a sharp object as your body responds by immediately shifting your weight to minimize any damage. It is difficult to describe this skill until you experience it. Once it is honed, however, it will allow you to run on very difficult terrain with limited visibility.

I have advanced to the point of being able to run on fairly technical leaf-covered trails barefoot. If I do not see an object, my brain has enough trail experience to be able to immediately adjust and shift to prevent injury. You too will develop this skill as you spend more time on various terrains.

It can also be useful to learn your local plant life. For example, I live in an area where oak trees litter the ground with acorns. When I see an oak tree along a sidewalk or trail, I also expect to see acorns. Another example are dead raspberry plants that sometimes scattered the ground near raspberry patches. I will avoid these areas since it is difficult to see the dead plants on the ground. Bottom line, it pays to have knowledge of your surroundings.

Activity—Debris Drill

 The purpose of the debris drill is to practice your ability to run through a field of objects that could be harmful. Part of this critical skill is the ability to create a mental map of the terrain in front of you.

Find an open area free of obstacles like furniture or stairs where you can spread debris across the floor. Use something non-injurious like small pebbles, building blocks, or small stuffed animals. Avoid things such as thumb tacks, broken glass, or live animals. Look at the debris pattern for a moment. Close your eyes and try to walk across the floor based only on the mental map in your head.

This sharpens your ability to move your feet to the clear areas based on your mental map. It also sharpens your ability to adjust your body weight when you do step on something.

Concept—Increasing Speed and/or Distance

 Learning the art and science of barefoot running is an exercise in patience. While the basic form required to run injury-free is fairly intuitive, mastering the form takes time—something that can be disheartening to the new barefoot runner. Let's say a conventional runner is accustomed to running a certain weekly mileage or regularly runs at a fast pace. This is not possible when learning to run barefoot.

When transitioning, some may opt to continue their shod

running. While this can be a good pacifying strategy for the inner competitor, new barefoot runners will eventually cross a threshold where running in their old shoes will be uncomfortable at best; injurious at worst. Often at this critical time a new barefoot runner will question their decision to run without shoes. They may have been an accomplished runner but now can only muster short, slow distances barefoot.

The progression of speed and distance is very slow when beginning barefoot running. Finding a form that works well for you can be difficult requiring considerable time and patience. Once found, the buildup of mileage is slow as your body acclimates to the new style of running. Bones, muscles, tendons, and ligaments need time to adapt from the time they were imprisoned in the foot coffins (thanks again for that analogy, Barefoot Ted). Run too far or too fast and you will likely develop soft-tissue injuries, such as the dreaded "top of the foot" pain or worse, you may develop a stress fracture.

It is critically important to go slow while learning and adapting. It is necessary to exercise patience to learn and adapt. This period can range from annoying to frustrating to downright depressing. It will feel as if you will never regain your old speed or distance. Don't worry, there IS light at the end of the tunnel!

Once you find a form that works for you AND you allow your feet, ankles, legs, and the rest of your body to adapt to the feeling of losing the shoes, you will be free to increase both distance and pace. You still need to exercise caution and follow reasonable guidelines, but the rate of improvement is NOT linear. At some point you will find yourself running longer and/or faster, finally running more weekly mileage because you are less prone to injury—without the anchors tied to your feet.

If you were a runner prior to starting this journey, you WILL recapture your previous abilities. It just takes patience. Like the tortoise and the hare. The hare may get out of the blocks faster, but the tortoise always wins.

Puncture wounds and cuts are two of the inherent dangers of barefoot running. Though not as significant as some anti-barefoot running naysayers claim, the danger is real. I have been running barefoot for thousands of miles on all types of surfaces, in all weather conditions, at any time of day or night. In all that time, I have stepped on only approximately five thorns and one glass sliver.

This danger is easy to minimize. As I have discussed before, simply watch your path. Almost all potentially dangerous materials are easy to spot. In the event you do step on something, your body's reaction will minimize the likelihood of driving the object into your foot.

Glass is a common fear. This is understandable... it's sharp! In my experience, most glass found along roads or sidewalks is surprisingly dull. If the glass has been exposed to the environment or traffic, the sharp edges will almost immediately be ground to a harmless edge. Of course, I would always advise you to avoid any glass, even if it is harmless.

In the event you do get a thorn, sliver, or other object embedded in your foot, you should be able to remove it yourself. If it is severe, seek medical attention. But if it is not severe, usually a pair of tweezers, some anti-bacterial ointment, and an adhesive bandage is all that will be needed to fix the problem.

If you cannot grasp the object with tweezers, place a dab of Elmer's Glue over the object. Allow it to thoroughly dry, and then peel the glue dot off. Many times, the object will adhere to the glue and can easily be removed.

Ten Barefoot Running Tips

1. A necklace worn around your neck can be a handy training tool. As you run, the necklace should remain more or less stationary. If it bounces up and down, you are probably overstriding. And if it sways from side to side, your upper body is moving too much or your arms are moving across your body.

2. If you are running on an asphalt road that is too rough, running on the painted white line will often be smoother. The lines can also be cooler in hot weather.

3. Carrying a foot care kit can be helpful should you injure yourself. My kit includes alcohol wipes for sterilization, tweezers for removing slivers or thorns, two adhesive bandages, and super glue to apply to minor cuts.

4. If running with a jogging stroller, stand toward one side so you can see debris in your path. For example, stand behind and to the left of the stroller while pushing with your right arm. This will give you an unobstructed view of the path to the left of the stroller.

5. Sand can be used as an indicator of good form. Run across a patch of sand. If your footprint is almost perfectly flat, you are effectively lifting your foot (this is good) but if there is a divot at the front of your foot, you are pushing off with your toes (this is bad).

6. If you find yourself over-analyzing your form, do something to distract yourself. Personally, I prefer to eat. Small candy works well. Others have reported success with listening to music, running with a partner and engaging in conversation, or running with a dog.

7. When running on a flat surface for a long time, the repetitive motions can cause the same muscles to work repeatedly. This will also apply the same stress to bones, tendons, ligaments, etc. Doing anything to add variety

can be very useful. This would include running through a short section of grass along sidewalks, running on the gravel on the side of an asphalt road, or even jumping on or over obstacles along your path.

8. When running in cold temperatures, your feet will lose sensation. Most people will regain sensation as blood flow increases later in the run. To help speed the warm-up process, make sure you dress in warm clothing. Long pants work much better than shorts. Also, your feet will stay warmer as long as you are moving. Avoid stopping.

9. If you ever have to enter a store barefoot and they have a "no barefoot" policy, act as if you were wearing shoes. If you are walking with confidence, few people will notice. Those that do notice will be unlikely to confront you if you act as if you are doing nothing wrong.

10. This one is a bit radical. For those of us that have to wear shoes in the winter, our feet will lose some of their adaptation to walking and running over rough terrain. You can maintain some degree of adaptation by adding a tablespoon of fine gravel or kitty litter to your shoes. When spring comes, you gain your "summer feet" much quicker.

More Tips from Barefoot Runner Evelia Huack

I don't worry or think too much about what my feet are doing.

I know that by keeping my body relaxed the rest of my body immediately follows.

I know that what works for me might not work for others. If one gives the body time to get accustomed to the new running style it will not let you down.

When out on a run I focus my attention on my surroundings, it helps me to relax and makes my runs much more enjoyable.

I truly enjoy the freedom that BFR gives me. There are no limitations as to how far I can go.

Tips

Introduce speed work once you have
developed an endurance base.

Setting overly-ambitious goals usually leads
to frustration and failure.

Stop imposing you own limitations.

It's very important to start slow and easy.

Just let your feet do what they do best.

And my favorite is ... relax and run.

Advanced Barefoot Running
Becoming an expert ...

Congratulations! You are making great progress. As you develop as a barefoot runner, you may want to begin racing, trail running, or training in poor weather conditions. This section covers topics for advanced barefoot runners. Each element requires the development of a new set of skills. Just like the skills you have learned up to this point, you should exercise patience in your development. Remember to train smart and listen to your body.

Concept—Racing

 One of the first questions new barefoot runners ask when jumping to organized racing is where to attach the timing chip (or other timing device). I use an MP3 player arm band around my ankle and attach the timing chip to that. HOWEVER, placement there may be too high to register on some timing mats.

If there aren't many other racers, you can listen for the audible "beep" as you cross the mat.

Pretty much any device will work to attach the timing device to your leg or foot—obviously avoiding staples and super glue. There are some people who use triathlon straps while others prefer to duct tape the chip to their foot. Use your imagination!

In any race, it is important to know your limitations. If you have a desired goal time over any given distance, be sure you have trained for that particular pace. Remember to maintain good form throughout. In the heat of competition, it is easy to allow your form to suffer. I have been guilty of pushing myself harder than I should have, and injuries have resulted.

One ever-important thing to remember: ALWAYS thank all of the volunteers. They are sacrificing their time for you so show your appreciation. Never complain or scold a volunteer. You are representing all barefoot runners so show everyone you are having fun out there.

As for competition, it is always good to compete against yourself. Set goals and always strive for self-improvement. Don't get caught up in beating those around you. All too often, we get swept up in what others are doing and lose sight of what made running fun in the first place. If winning is important to you, strive to be the best you can be. If that results in your beating others, so be it. Always allow victory to be a by-product of accomplishing your own goals.

Enjoy running for the sake of running, not the rewards of winning a race. George Sheehan said, "Once you have decided that winning isn't everything, you become a winner." This is the secret to longevity in running. You will never burn out if you love the process instead of the outcome.

Running on trails is a wonderful experience! That said, running barefoot on trails can be an even better treat. How better to make the connection with nature than running barefoot through the woods?

Running barefoot on trails does require specific skills:

First, a runner MUST be adept at forming a mental map of the terrain in front of them. And second, they must have fully developed the strength and skill to "hop" around debris.

On trails your foot placement and stride distance will vary resulting in an inconsistent gait. Without proper strengthening, this will quickly lead to fatigue which can increase the likelihood of injury. To have success on the trails the runner should have developed, through experience, the ability to immediately shift their weight in the event they step on a sharp object. When running barefoot on roads, runners quickly learn to avoid sharp objects, though stepping on tiny pebbles and other such debris is inevitable. Finally, the runner has to develop a gait that will allow them to pick their feet up high enough to clear the obstacles on the trail. All the above skills can be developed in a relatively short time.

To develop your trail running skills, it is first necessary to develop good form. Before advancing to this level you should feel comfortable running several miles pain-free on roads. Start slowly on trails beginning with barefoot trail walking. Gradually mix in VERY slow running. As your skills develop, you can increase both pace and distance. Using this formula, it is entirely possible to adapt to running on any terrain.

Be aware that some people recommend you begin barefoot running on trails for one of two reasons: The softness of the terrain or that by avoiding rough terrain you build skills faster. I disagree with both reasons. While the relative "softness" of the terrain is less likely to cause blisters, it is also more likely to hide flaws in your form. As for rough terrain building skills faster, always having to avoid rough spots will increase the amount of time needed to find your own unique ideal form.

Trail running should be considered an advanced form of barefoot running and should only be attempted after several months of barefoot running.

Concept—Extreme Weather

 Barefoot running in ideal conditions is usually pretty straight-forward. However, sometimes you may encounter conditions that are less-than-ideal for barefoot running. That said, for the most part, minimalist runners do not have a major problem with these conditions. Some of these less than ideal conditions are addressed below.

Hot Surfaces—Running in hot weather can be a difficult task in itself for all runners. For the barefoot runner, it poses the special challenge of having to run on a hot surface. A barefoot runner may also encounter this problem on some treadmills, because the deck will heat up as friction increases. Generally, asphalt is the worst surface for hot, sunny days. My personal preference is to avoid it and run early in the morning or later evening. If you must run on hot asphalt, there is a certain degree of acclimation that can occur.

Start by running VERY short distances on hot asphalt, then slowly increase that distance over the course of several days and weeks. CAUTION—DO NOT ATTEMPT THIS IF THE ASPHALT IS HOT ENOUGH TO BURN YOU! I live in a relatively mild climate, but those living in hot climates should either avoid hot asphalt by running in the morning, evening, or at night; or wear minimalist shoes. If you can fry an egg on the pavement, it's too hot. Remember this tip: if you are in a pinch and must run on hot asphalt without being able to acclimate to it, try running on the white line. It will be significantly cooler than the black asphalt. Be careful of traffic, however!

Cold Surfaces—Cold weather presents the exact opposite challenge. If the temperatures are above freezing it is possible to slowly acclimate to the cold. However, the cold will reduce the sensation of your feet on the ground resulting in less feedback going to your brain. If you feel this is too much of an injury risk, I recommend wearing some type of minimalist shoe.

Early in my barefoot running career, I wore aqua socks layered with thermal wool socks underneath. Today, I prefer Vibram KSOs® with a pair of Injinji® toe socks underneath. In either case, it allows for a decent approximation of barefoot running. During the winter months, I will also do limited barefoot running on treadmills to help maintain the "feel" of running barefoot.

Running on ice and snow can help perfect your form because the slippery conditions require near-perfect form to maintain balance. If you have a tendency to over-stride, push off, or have any other obvious flaws, running on very slippery surfaces will be nearly impossible. When running on slippery surfaces, please exercise extreme caution. Falling is not only a possibility, it is probable.

To keep my barefoot running form during the winter, I spend as much time as possible running barefoot indoors.

I have been experimenting with some barefoot running outdoors in the winter. Interestingly, the early returns are promising. While running in snow is initially uncomfortable (the cold hurts), my feet do seem to warm up to the point of being able to "feel" the terrain well enough to navigate fairly technical trails.

Wet Surfaces—Rain is usually not an issue unless you are exposed to it for a long period of time. After a few hours, wet skin tends to become macerated, which greatly increases the likelihood of blistering. Wearing a minimalist shoe is recommended for long distances in the rain. Alternatively, you can counteract the effect if you allow your feet to dry periodically. This can be difficult in a race, but may be an acceptable solution when training.

Running in the Dark—Visibility is the obvious issue when running in the dark barefoot making it nearly impossible to see the terrain ahead. As such, you will not be able to avoid potentially hazardous obstacles. The solution is to use some sort of illumination which may consist of a headlamp, handheld flashlight or a combination of both.

For barefoot runners, I recommend a handheld flashlight versus a headlamp because the light source for a headlamp is close to your eyes making trail debris difficult to see. If you hold a handheld light near your waist the shadows are cast at an angle that is very easy to see.

If you would prefer to keep your hands free, you can use the common ultrarunner trick of affixing the headlamp to your chest or your waist. This will avoid the problem of poor angles.

If running on roads with little debris, use one or the other. On technical trails, use both at the same time. The more you can illuminate the area ahead of yourself, the greater your ability to avoid trouble. Also remember to wear bright, reflective clothing and try to avoid routes with automobile traffic.

Winter Running by Barefoot Rick Roeber

It became a test of my will and body. My barefoot running began in the Fall and it quickly became cold here in the Midwest. However, I was undeterred. Even though it was below freezing many days when I ran, the feedback from my body told me that I was running "right". I felt a gratification after each run that I had not felt before. The blisters, the cold toes, the dry and cracking skin on my feet did not keep me from barefoot running. I would heal up and be right back at it, sometimes in the ice and snow.

I believe that it is possible to run for years and years barefoot, regardless of weather. I don't believe I will ever be incredibly fast at barefoot running, but for me, that's not the point. Longevity, that's what it's all about for me. I would like to, one day, know that I was one of the few who had kept at barefoot running and had set records in most barefoot miles run, most marathons, most 5Ks, or any number of things measurable in the endurance sport of barefoot running. The key is not giving up but continuing to persevere—getting out there daily and running my mileage. I am not looking for "flash in the pan" status because of my barefoot running. I do believe, however, that if I stick with it, the mileage, marathons, endurance running in snow and inclement weather will speak for itself.

Barefoot Rick Roeber
http://barefootrunner.org

This essay was reprinted with permission from Barefoot Rick Roeber. The original can be found here: http://barefootrunner.org/reflections/05reflections.htm.

Treadmills can be an effective tool to help new barefoot and minimalist shoe runners learn proper form. That said, there are a few concerns associated with treadmills.

The deck of most treadmills will heat up as speed and distance increase. This can generate enough heat to actually burn bare feet. If your treadmill does heat up, you have a few options.

You could move from one area of the deck to another. When I began barefoot running, I used this strategy identifying five "areas" on the treadmill deck that would be rotated. Since most of the heat was generated in the area I was running, moving around delayed the buildup of heat. The problem with this tactic was safety as I would occasionally step on the rail of the treadmill causing me to stumble.

The other solution is to wear minimalist shoes. While it is not the best condition for learning good form, it is better than not running.

The second major concern with treadmills has to do with abrasiveness. Most treadmill decks have a tendency to cause cuts and blisters. This seems to be an effect of the physics behind the moving belt making it more difficult to pick your foot up and place it down without experiencing some sort of shearing force.

Normally, barefoot running requires your foot to move vertically. Since the belt is moving, placing your foot straight down will result in some friction. You can overcome this by employing a concept known as "paw-back." Essentially, you want your foot to be moving backward as it touches the belt. If your foot is moving at the same speed, friction is dramatically reduced.

Unfortunately, paw-back is a difficult skill to master with the best solution being to simply start slow. Begin with walking and build up to slow running. With time, you will be able to tolerate faster speeds.

There is one obvious problem with the use of treadmills. If you learn to run barefoot using a treadmill, you will have some issues with running on non-moving surfaces. This is not a major issue as you will quickly adapt to running without paw-back, but it will require some practice. Do not attempt to run at a fast pace or over a long distance without first practicing non-treadmill running techniques.

Ultramarathons

Testing Human Potential

"Perhaps the genius of ultra running is its supreme lack of utility. It makes no sense in a world of space ships and supercomputers to run vast distances on foot. There is no money in it and no fame, frequently not even the approval of peers. But as poets, apostles and philosophers have insisted from the dawn of time, there is more to life than logic and common sense. The ultra runners know this instinctively. And they know something else that is lost on the sedentary. They understand, perhaps better than anyone, that the doors to the spirit will swing open with physical effort. In running such long and taxing distances they answer a call from the deepest realms of their being—a call that asks who they are."

—David Blaikie

Ultramarathons represent the extreme of human running ability. In their 2004 *Nature* article, Drs. Dennis Bramble and Daniel Lieberman presented a convincing theory that humans evolved to run long distances based on unique anatomical and physiological traits. This article was one of the influential pieces featured in McDougall's *Born to Run*. Ultramarathons are the ultimate test of our unique abilities.

The length of an Ultramarathon is officially any distance greater than the standard 26.2 mile (42.195K) marathon and include 50K, 50-mile, 100K, and 100-mile distances. It is entirely possible to reach these distances both in minimalist shoes and barefoot. I fell in love with ultras immediately. The sense of camaraderie among ultrarunners is second to none. If you decide to try these events, some of these ultra tips may be useful.

It is important to train in similar conditions as the race for which you are training. If the race has hills, train on hills. If the trail has a lot of roots and rocks, train on trails with plenty of roots and rocks. This is especially important because you have to allow your feet to acclimate to the unique challenges you will encounter.

When going either barefoot or wearing minimalist shoes, it is important to know the course prior to training runs. If you cannot run the course prior to the race, try to get reports from other barefoot runners.

Train in a range of temperatures you MAY experience on race day by conducting research to determine the hottest, coldest, and average temperatures. Be prepared to use different strategies and wear different clothing depending on the potential conditions.

Weight training really helps, especially with muscle fatigue and recovery time. Ideally, your weight training routine should prepare you for the specific conditions encountered when running long distances. See the chapter on Training Plans (page 121) for specific information on my own training regime.

I've found rest and recovery to be the most important components of any training program. Be aware that training takes a toll on your body and rest days are necessary to allow your body to heal. As someone more knowledgeable than myself once said, "Being under-prepared is better than being over-trained."

Figure out how much you need to drink based on various levels of effort in different weather conditions. I've made the mistake of drinking too much in cool weather resulting in lost time urinating excessively. In one particular 50-mile race, I lost nearly an hour due to that.

Practice dealing with issues that may arise (blisters, chafing, nausea, etc.) so you can confront them as they arise during the run. The best way to prepare for these possible problems is to experience them in your training runs. I have purposely avoided using anti-chafing lubrication, ran faster than I should have, and even consumed a large fast-food meal prior to a run in order to artificially create problems that I've solved on the fly. Now if I'm presented with those same challenges during a run, I have practiced the solutions.

Test A LOT of different foods, gels, and sport drinks to find what works for you. After the miles start to pile up, you may find some foods more palatable than others. For myself, I enjoy sweet foods early in a race, but cannot tolerate them after about 20 miles. My fail-safe go-to food when all else fails is chia seeds taken with water or diluted wine. It is an odd combination, but works well for me.

Racing

Start slow! The greatest mistake you can make is to start too fast, then bonk later in the race. There are different strategies people use for ultras. Some will run at a slow, steady pace as long as possible while others will schedule regular walking breaks.

Walk all hills. It is a good opportunity to change your stride and help distribute fatigue. Running hills, especially early in a race, is a recipe for disaster.

Eat early and often. Adequate caloric intake will help later in the race. Different runners can tolerate more or less food with the average seeming to be around 250 calories per hour. For myself, in some races I will consume upwards of 450 calories per hour.

Stay adequately hydrated. You should know how much you need to drink based on training. I also use urine frequency and color as a gauge. If I am urinating more than once every 90 minutes, I am drinking too much. If my urine is very yellow or dark, I am drinking too little.

Keep your electrolyte intake balanced to your fluid intake. Consuming too much salt usually causes gastrointestinal distress, consuming too little can cause hyponatremia (possibly fatal). I prefer an electrolyte supplement like Succeed S! Caps.

Any area of your body that protrudes or experiences some friction can chafe. This includes thighs, groin, toes, armpits, nipples, etc. Chafing can be difficult because you may not recognize it until it has already developed. Find a good anti-chafing product such as Sportslick, BodyGlide, or SportWax. If you do develop chafing, baby diaper rash cream can be an effective remedy.

Running ultras usually involves some degree of pain. Learn to manage it without drugs. Both ibuprofen and acetaminophen can result in acute health troubles if misused. Consult your physician.

Repeating a positive mantra, like "I feel great!" can be a very effective distracter.

Plan for potential problems based on your experiences while training (blisters, chafing, cuts/bruises, bugs, rain, nausea, diarrhea, etc.) Having a plan going into a race may help prevent a DNF (Did Not Finish).

Taper! Tapering is the progressive cessation of activities to allow your body to heal. Give your body at least a few days off prior to your race. I start decreasing the intensity of my workouts at least two weeks prior to 50-milers and up to three weeks before 100-milers including one week of near-zero mileage immediately prior to the race. This assures that I am healthy and injury-free at the start of the race.

Don't forget to smile, no explanation is needed.

Gear

Test all of your gear prior to the race. This includes clothing, anti-chafing measures, anti-blister measures, shoes (for you Luddites that insist on wearing them …), hydration systems, food, etc. Everything you rely upon for a race is a potential problem. The more familiar you are with each variable, the less likely it will become a problem.

Be prepared if gear breaks, gets lost or is ineffective. Have a contingency plan for everything. If you are using a crew, make sure your crew is aware of your contingency plan.

One of the best ways to prepare for running ultramarathons is to volunteer at races. Watching other runners can be an invaluable teaching experience.

Serving as a crew member or pacer can also be beneficial. Crew members meet runners at various points during the run. Their job is to resupply their runners and help solve problems that may arise. Pacers actually run with their runner for parts of the race. It is their job to keep the runner on pace to finish, provide motivation, find the trail, or any other task the runner is incapable of doing on their own.

Body Efficiency

Training barefoot has allowed my body to become more efficient. When running 50 or 100 miles, wasting energy with improper form can add hours to your finishing time and worse yet cause serious injury. Barefoot running is an invaluable tool towards learning to run the way our bodies have evolved to function.

Patrick Sweeney
http://bourbonfeet.com

Other Topics

Dealing with "Hecklers" and Common Comebacks

One concern many new barefoot runners have is the fear of being a social outcast. It is a legitimate fear because some of the lay-public see barefoot running as absolutely crazy. Despite the increased popularity in recent years, we are still a minority. For years the public has been fed by shoe company propaganda and little, if any, working knowledge about the benefits of barefoot running.

Other runners present a different problem. In my experiences, they fit into one of four categories: the non-running lay-public and, inquisitive, amazed, or hostile runners. Each group is unique and requires a slightly different approach.

• *The non-running lay-public*—This is the fun group because they see barefoot running as super-human. To them running itself is a Herculean task and running barefoot is even more so. They are likely to exclaim, "Look, that guy has no shoes." A simply way to respond is with a humorous reply like, "I woke up late and forgot them at home!" Be careful and courteous with this group because if they are watching you run, they have some interest in running and with encouragement could become runners one day.

• *The inquisitive running peers*—This is the group that could be future converts. These are the people who approach you before, during, or after races asking questions and seeming interested. Every barefoot runner loves this group; they give us external validation. Always point them toward sources of additional information such as websites or blogs about barefoot theory (shameless plug—recommend they visit http:// barefootrunninguniversity.com). They will usually have a lot of questions; do your best to answer every one. The goal is to convince these people that barefoot running will work for them.

• *The amazed peers*—This is a strange group. They are generally skeptical about barefoot running but may be interested in the benefits. These are the people that approach you after a race and say, "Wow! I can't believe you just ran that race barefoot!" This group could be future converts as well. When encountering them always act humble and talk about how lucky you are to have had the opportunity to run such a wonderful race. Be genuinely nice and tell them they did a great job. Never push barefoot running on this group. At the next race, there's a good possibility they will be in the "inquisitive" group as long as you don't do anything to turn them off to barefoot running. This is why you should ALWAYS remember to smile!

• *The hostile peers*—This is the tough group. They are almost always young males, perhaps middle age, who are passionate about their shoes. They sincerely believe shoes are the variable that has brought them whatever measure of success they have achieved. While there is a tendency to ignore them, instead, allow your performance to speak for itself. Try engaging them in discussion using self-depreciating humor. It tends to disarm their hostility and allows them to see you for who you are. Your goal is not convert but to plant the barefoot seed. It may be several years before they think about barefoot running again, but they will. Perhaps an an injury will happen or maybe reading *Born to Run* will bring them around. They may even be exposed to barefoot running by friends or family. Whatever the case, do not disregard these people because *every* runner could later on become a barefoot runner.

As time passes, the acceptance of barefoot running has increased. When I first began my barefoot journey, the vast majority of runners were of the "hostile" variety. Today, most seem to have migrated to the "inquisitive" camp. Part of this migration is due to the increase in barefoot awareness and part of it has to do with the quality of the character of barefoot runners. As trailblazers it is critically important to be a good ambassador for barefoot running. Every person you encounter has the potential to be a barefoot runner. Never forget that.

Those who have not yet tried barefoot running will often cite a lack of time to devote to training. To solve this time-management issue many recommend a regimented training schedule. However, for myself, I prefer a less organized approach. Rather than searching for opportunities to train, instead I turn everything I can into a training opportunity.

To start, at home I always walk around barefoot to help strengthen my feet and hone my tactile sense. It allows me the opportunity to practice walking with a midfoot strike versus a heel strike.

When weather allows, I walk around outside our house barefoot. The concrete sidewalk, asphalt driveway, woodchip landscaping, and grass lawn provide plenty of sensory stimulation for my feet. I also practice some of the drills casually by routinely picking up debris with my feet. Throughout the course of a day I'm always looking for opportunities to test and practice these skills.

Most places of work present a potential difficulty. However, if your career allows you to go barefoot, indulge. Otherwise, there may be some viable options such as wearing only socks or minimalist shoes such as those by Terra Plana, Feelmax, or Vibram. In the event you are the employer perhaps you can consider loosening up your policies on shoes. If you have the power to be an agent of change, embrace the opportunity.

Iskiate

In his book, *Born to Run*, Chris McDougall discusses the habits of the Tarahumara Indians of Copper Canyon, Mexico. One of their staples are chia seeds mixed with water and a hint of lime juice. The resulting *iskiate* is renowned for its usefulness as a mid-run fuel.

I was skeptical of this concoction until forced to try it during the 2009 Hallucination 100-mile run (find the details in the race report later in the book). Since that run I have experimented with various methods to ingest chia while running. At one point in my research, my friends Andy Grosvenor and Kate Kift even suggested using wine instead of water as a liquid base for the iskiate.

In May of 2010, I actually tried this combination for the Mind the Ducks 12-hour ultramarathon in Rochester, New York. Due to New York's liquor laws, I was only able to procure

Mike's Hard Lemonade which is a carbonated malt beverage with a slight lemon taste.

Throughout that race, I used a combination of Mike's and chia to maintain adequate caloric intake by pouring about two ounces of Mike's into a cup and adding a scoop of chia seeds then immediately consuming it. I did this about once an hour.

The use of a small amount of alcohol during a long run is very controversial and not something I recommend others try. I just wanted to report that during that run it gave me some positive benefits.

Diet and Race Food

Along with questions about iskiate, people often ask about my diet. My diet can be summed up with two terms: *variety* and *moderation.*

I try to eat many different foods. When shopping at the grocery store, I use a simple guideline of buying foods found around the perimeter of the store and in a variety of colors. Food found around the perimeter of most stores will be fresh since fruits, vegetables, meats, dairy, and breads are found in these areas. The middle aisles of most stores contain processed foods such as canned vegetables, cookies, and potted meat. Anything that is prepared via the "potted" method is less healthy.

I am also a food realist. As much as I would like to claim to adhere to a healthy diet, that would be a facade. I like food—including that which is healthy and that which is not. When I have an urge to eat I will usually indulge, though moderation is important when satisfying these urges. When eating something unhealthy, I will try limiting that portion to a size no larger than my fist. For me it is a simple but direct method of portion control.

I also look for patterns when I tend to overeat. For example, I tend to be an emotional eater. If I am experiencing an unusual level of stress, I have a tendency to overeat. It is also something I'll do when I'm bored. For me the trick to preventing or minimizing overeating is to understand, predict, and correct the triggers that cause the behavior. When I keep myself busy, drink water, and exercise, it greatly limits my own overeating.

While racing, I tend to favor high-calorie whole foods and shy away from the engineered foods some runners use, such as gels. Through experimentation, I've found foods such as hot dogs, hamburgers, and donuts work well. While it is not a popular strategy, it works for me. During longer runs, the sweetness of most gels is unpalatable and whole foods are much easier to consume.

Bad Runs

A "bad run" is any run where something does not feel "right" and manifests itself in a variety of ways. You may feel fatigued or your feet and legs may seem unusually heavy. Other symptoms may include sleepiness or a variety of dull pains throughout your body.

Runners, as if following an unwritten rule, do not talk about bad runs. When I began running, it was my assumption that I was the only person who experienced bad runs, as other runners would gush over how wonderful each and every step felt. It was as if I was the only runner that didn't experience the "muffins wrapped in rainbows" runs everyone else apparently experienced.

Oddly, my wife Shelly and I didn't talk about our experiences with bad runs for years. Perhaps we became adept at sensing when the other was having a bad run and then stuck by the runners code and remained silent.

In 2009, I had the opportunity to listen to a lecture from ultrarunning legend Scott Jurek whom I consider to be a role model mostly because of his humble, gracious demeanor. Scott embodies everything I believe ultrarunning should be. During that lecture, Scott talked about having difficulties during the race and shared that even the elite runners have extreme moments of self-doubt where they are tempted to quit.

For me, this was a major epiphany. When Scott Jurek, a world class ultrarunner, talked about bad runs he was affirming the lows we all experience. This opened a floodgate of discussion between Shelly and me as if we had finally received permission to discuss this frequently-occurring phenomenon.

Okay, so we all experience bad runs. Now, how do we deal with the bad run? There are really two options:

Option 1: Stop. Most runners do not find this option acceptable because it is likely to cause some guilt or anxiety and they see it as a personal failure or an admission of weakness. Or so we think. Sometimes I do stop. If, after the first mile or two, it does not feel right, I will pull the plug.

Based on past experiences, these negative feelings are usually an indicator of a problem. If that problem is physical in nature, we run a greater risk of injuring ourselves. So if I feel I am not "right" physically, I will postpone the run. I may try the same run later in the day, or I may skip it altogether.

Option 2: Fight through it. This is the popular advice most other runners will give because fighting through adversity is a popular theme in our culture. We've all watched the film *Rocky* where Rocky Balboa gets punched in the head repeatedly by Apollo Creed while refusing to surrender. While it makes for a good story, how smart is it to get punched in the head 200 times in one night? Probably not that smart. Similarly, it is not always wise to push yourself when a physical or mental problem may exist.

Of course, sometimes I do push on. Occasionally the desire to run is greater than the negative feelings. If, for example, my children are especially challenging on the day of a bad run, I may push through the negativity just for the sake of silence.

It is important to note that if you decide to push on, be careful. Be especially mindful of your physical state. Try going a little slower or maybe try eating or drinking something. Dehydration or glycogen depletion can be contributing factors to the "bad run" feeling. However, be prepared to stop the run if your state worsens.

Your brain has more power over your physical state than most realize. The power of positive thought can easily turn a bad run into a good run. I will often use an oft-repeated phrase as a positive affirmation which can be shockingly effective. Here are some of the phrases I use:

- "I know I am a good runner!"
- "I've done this run in the past, I can do it again!"
- "I have felt much worse than this in past runs and still finished!"
- "I feel great!"

While they may sound silly, *they really do work*. It is not necessary to repeat the mantras aloud, though some prefer to do so. Figure out which works for you, then unapologetically stick with it.

Introducing social pressure can be another method to overcoming bad runs. If you have other people to run with, their presence may be the subtle push required to change your mood.

Regardless of your methods, always remember to be vigilant about monitoring your body for injury. This is especially true while running in a social setting. Many of my own injuries have resulted from the stupidity of trying to keep up with a speedy running partner when I was physically ill-prepared.

Barefoot Running: A Podiatrist's Perspective

For hundreds of thousands of years, human feet have taken us from point A to point B, and only recently have they become encased, on a daily basis, in supportive footwear. Our feet have evolved to be tough and resilient. In fact, even after enduring all kinds of high-impact activity or even serious trauma, our feet often continue to function adequately.

However, in all my years as a podiatry student and podiatric surgical resident, my professors rarely, if ever, discussed any type of barefoot activity. Instead, they spent hundreds of hours teaching the importance of supportive footwear, arch supports, and the

Holy Grail of podiatric medicine, the foot orthotic. An orthotic is a custom-made arch support formed from a mold of a person's foot intended to help realign their foot into a more optimal, correct position, and with some very rare exceptions, podiatrists believe most of their patients need them.

But research is starting to suggest that all this extra cushioning may be making it difficult for feet to stand on their own. So after nearly twenty years in practice, I began to question the prescribed doctrine: Do feet really need all this support?

What Do Scientists Say About Barefoot Running?

The scientific literature does not prove—at least not yet—that barefoot activity or barefoot running is better for you. But the preliminary findings, when taken together and compared with the detrimental effects of supportive shoes, trend toward the inevitable conclusion: barefoot is better.

Most compelling are epidemiological studies showing that populations in the world that have generally walked barefoot or worn only sandals suffer from significantly fewer foot problems and deformities. Essentially, the constant pressure of shoes on our feet and toes cause the bones, joints, and tissues to adapt to the shoe. Even with the widest of shoes, you will notice that the toe area often curves inward at the great toe. The effect of this inward curve makes the shoe's toe area rounded and, perhaps, more stylish. But over time, the shoe's pressure on the great toe will cause it to drift toward the smaller toes and a painful bunion deformity (a bump) on the inside of the foot may develop.

Biomechanical reports on supportive footwear reveal that it often takes over for most of the muscles in our feet, which weakens them and makes these muscles unnecessary. Shoe companies and arch support makers may frame this as a good thing: your muscles do not need to work as hard, if at all. However, next time you slip on supportive shoes, remind yourself of the old saying, "use it or lose it." Your shoes are acting like tiny coffins for most of your feet muscles, causing them to weaken, and even atrophy. With regards to running, no solid proof shows that shoes prevent injuries, and according to some studies, the injury rate for shoe-wearing runners may be as high as 79 percent.

Lastly, when I looked at all the peer-reviewed journal articles in existence that compared barefoot and shoe-wearing running, I found that nearly all of them favored going bare. Although the scientific literature shows a correlation with running shoes to injury, I could not find one article on the detrimental effects of barefoot activity.

What Do Other Podiatrists Say About Barefoot Running?

In 2008, the American Podiatric Medical Association (APMA) issued the press release, "Podiatrists Urge Americans to Think Twice Before Going Barefoot." In the release, Dr. Ross Taubman, president of the APMA, stated, "It's always safer to put on some kind of protective footwear every time you step outside."

Oddly, the release goes on to say children learning to walk should not wear protective footwear because the child's foot needs to grow normally and develop its musculature and strength. One has to wonder, if the APMA believes shoes are problematic for muscle development in children, why wouldn't shoes cause similar problems for adults? All muscles need exercise on a regular basis throughout our life—not just in childhood—so they stay healthy and strong. Shouldn't we continue to exercise our foot muscles beyond childhood? The obvious answer is yes. Since the APMA recommends keeping shoes off children's feet for muscle strength and development, then perhaps adults should do this too.

Recently, someone asked me what it would take for the medical community to endorse barefoot running. My answer was simple: It will never happen. For one, physicians have a financial stake in arch supports and orthotics. But there's more to it than that. Health practitioners who have spent their life believing that feet need help and support can't suddenly accept that feet, with proper training, can make it on their own.

Further, beyond health practitioners, the general population still, for the most part, believes feet need support, stability, and plenty of cushioning. Until people begin having faith in their remarkable, strong, and resilient feet, ankles, and entire lower extremities, and begin asking questions—to themselves, their doctors, and the shoe companies—the medical system and footwear manufacturers will continue to feed them the same information they always have.

Final Thoughts on Barefoot Running

After I read Christopher McDougall's book, *Born to Run*, and his account of the Tarahumara Indians who routinely run dozens of miles a day in flimsy sandal-like shoes—without injury—I took the leap from armchair scientist to barefoot runner.

Transitioning from my own custom-made orthotics and expensive running shoes to barefoot was not easy. Back then, I didn't have this book or any other resource to guide me. It was trial and error, and I did get hurt by doing too much too fast. But, I didn't give up.

Eventually, I became comfortable running in minimalist shoes, and amazingly, my years of off-and-on heel pain (plantar fasciitis) went away (and to this day, it has not come back!). My feet and ankles are stronger, and, even better, my legs, thighs, and buttocks are leaner and firmer. I have better posture, too.

I love to run and plan to continue running for many, many years ... in my minimalist shoes.

By Michael Nirenberg, DPM
www.friendlyfootcare.com and www.americaspodiatrist.com

Running with Others

One of the joys of running comes from the camaraderie of running with other people. The same holds true for barefoot runners though there are a few issues that arise.

Not everyone is barefoot-friendly. It is important to find a running partner or group that is accepting of your running barefoot. Surrounding yourself with negative input and attitudes will only inhibit and sabotage the process of learning. Some people can be very defensive about their decision to run in shoes. Who can blame them? They probably spend hundreds of dollars per year on shoes.

If you run with an overly-negative person or a group with one or two negative people, find new running partners or learn to ignore them. Your success will provide all the ammunition you need to silence their negativity and in my experience is the best way to counter critics.

Pacing is another issue that sometimes arises when you decide to run with others. It is critically important to restrain yourself early in the learning process. By running with another person who is faster or runs longer distances, can dramatically increase the temptation to do too much too soon. If the other person runs faster, I would suggest finding a small loop course such as a high school track for runs. This will allow each of you to run at your own pace while still maintaining some contact.

For those running partners who go longer distances, try running only accompanying them for a portion of their run. Let them start earlier or continue to run longer after you finish. If you are running together for security reasons, a loop course works as a good solution. You can wait for them as they finish the remainder of their run.

The Doubtful Spouse/Partner

I am very lucky because Shelly has always accepted and supported my barefoot running endeavors. Perhaps she instinctively knew I was on the cutting edge of something truly great, or maybe that is what I want to believe. In reality, she probably just chalked it up to my eccentric nature.

Regardless, I have benefitted from her support. Many of the new barefoot runners have not enjoyed that level of understanding. Our spouses can be unwavering pillars that help us reach our potential or can be harsh critics that subvert our dreams and ideas. In the event your partner falls in the latter category, there are some tips to help sway their opinions.

First, lead by example. If they are a runner, this is probably easy. Do your thing, let them do theirs. If at some point they suffer an injury you may be able to convince them that their running shoes may have caused the injury.

Second, educate yourself about the merits of barefoot and minimalist shoe running AND the merits of shod running. Both have pros and cons. Learn them and be able to calmly discuss the issues. When your spouse voices something critical of barefoot running, be prepared to provide an intelligent response. Aside from the information contained in this book, study the resources provided at the end. There are many great websites available.

Third, provide them with information. For example, Shelly did not start barefoot running until she read *Born to Run*. Chris McDougall's book provides an excellent introduction to the fundamental theories that provide the foundation of barefoot running.

If all else fails, just have fun. Barefoot running is an absolute joy. Smile. Laugh. Lose your inhibitions and engross yourself in the experience. It is the single best advertisement for barefoot running.

What if I Still have Problems Running Barefoot?

If you worked through the techniques and drills found in this book and you are still having difficulty, you have several options. Though most people are, not everybody is well-suited for barefoot running. Or, sometimes ones learning style may differentiate from my teaching style. If that is the case, don't fret.

If my methods are not working for you at this point and you have spent many months trying to perfect them, there is little chance they will net positive results in the future. Therefore you may not be well-suited for running barefoot.

If my methods are not working for you then try other barefoot teachers. Ken Bob Saxton, Ted McDonald, Preston Curtis, and Michael Sander are four wonderful instructors whose methods vary slightly from mine and from each others. One of them may be a better match for you.

Lastly, try one of the running programs I mentioned earlier in the book: Good Form Running, ChiRunning, Evolution Running, and Pose. Each are very good and will teach you to run in a more efficient way. One of these may be better-suited for your particular learning style.

So, you wanna start running barefoot?

Firstly, before you begin, you want to evaluate what it is that is leading you to even accept the logic behind the concept of barefoot running. We all know that barefoot running has gotten a lot of attention lately. Much of it is valid and deserves your attention.

Yet, one must still ask: Is this a viable option for me?

Before you answer that question, let me explain why I think barefoot or minimal footwear running may not be good for you. It is not good if you are thinking it is some sort of cure-all that only requires taking off your shoes and starting to run injury-free without radical changes in the way you may have been thinking of running up to now.

If your running strategy has been about very specific time or distance goals, and you have been willing to push through pain to injury, then I would caution you: your barefeet will not allow you to continue this way.

Alas, the hallmark of my barefoot running philosophy is connectedness, mindfulness, presence.

Barefoot running is not about blocking or pushing through pain, or at least it shouldn't be. Rather it is about tuning-in to your own body's highly sophisticated set of integrated awareness systems, systems that communicate through feelings and senses that are being collected in real-time as you move. From my perspective, learning how to run well means learning how to tap into the feeling of running well, which more often than not requires baring the foot to get the full feel of what happens when you move.

However, even if you decide that barefoot is the route for you, take one step backward and realize you are most likely in the process of rehabilitating your feet and legs from years of being differently-abled, shoed, and cast. Atrophy, loss of range of motion, weakness, neglect, the foot has not been treated well lately. All the padding and support and protection has not led to stronger feet ... sadly.

So, the first key is to start slowly, incrementally and avoid over- exuberance, avoid being driven by your ego. Think orchard growing, not fast food. Think lifetime of development and growth. Think joy.

So, what are my secrets, what is it I share with clients who take my "Introduction to Barefoot Running Clinic"?

My goal is to get people to learn how to feel what good running feels like. I want them to develop a feeling for it. One of the primary feelings becomes an awareness of the texture and hardness of terrain and of impact. This awareness is the beginning.

To master this awareness, I have clients learn to move on hard surfaces first. Not focusing on distance or speed, I have my clients first walk and then trot on hard, fairly smooth surfaces. I work with them to focus on and begin to master three goals: quiet, quick, in balance.

The Three Goals

1. Master gentle, quiet, forefoot-centric landings, silent and smooth.

Learn to move with no hard edges and no pounding by learning how to have the impact of landing flow through the entire foot, starting in the forefoot and quickly spreading through the legs smoothly. Notice how silent your movement becomes. Imagine the movement of a big cat. Watch your dogs trot. Let them be models for tuned-in, flowing movement that wastes no energy on pound or sound.

2. Quicken your cadence. Running in bare feet encourages this naturally.

Some shoe runners are plodders. You can hear them coming. Lots of wasted energy on poorly timed impact. Quicker cadence ends up making sense when you realize that your ability to absorb and recoil energy through elasticity in your body dissipates quickly and is lost if not used. Learning how to get back in touch with the sweet spot of optimal recoil efficiency is easier to find when you can feel your feet, feeling that encourages a landing phase with foot more in line with your center of gravity (thinking about how you land if you jump down onto a hard surface in barefeet, not on your heels!). Overstriding is discouraged, nearly impossible barefooted.

3. Stable upright posture ... balanced head, core engaged, belly button pulled into the spine, no waist bending, head upright. The feeling of balance: relaxed, yet strong.

I think that good running can be judged aesthetically. It should look good, not painful. When you see someone moving or running well, it looks smooth and fluid and graceful and efficient. The opposite looks painful, when someone is hunched and stiff, robotic and plodding. Indeed efficient running is tall and stable, the upper body acting as the fulcrum from which the legs and arms can move freely with a serious lack of bouncing or swaying.

Ultimately my coaching goal is to help people perfect what I think of as a persistent hunt tro ... not purely about speed, but about smooth, flowing, efficient, sustainable movement, movement that leaves you ready to hunt another day.

Barefooting itself is all about mindfulness and presence. Running like a Monkey, not like a Robot. Aware of your body and your environment AT ALL TIMES.

Listen to your body ... learn to hear what it is telling you. Adjust accordingly. Advance accordingly.

Barefoot Ted McDonald
http://barefootted.com

Training Plans

Once you complete each of the stages covered in this book, you will be ready to run faster and longer. Many runners run races as a means of increasing their running abilities. To help in achieving your own running goals, I am including several of my own plans.

Please do not start any of these plans until you can run pain-free. I often recommend new barefoot runners avoid running on back-to-back days and these plans require running several days in a row. Because of this, you should exercise caution to avoid injury. If you do experience pain, take a day off. It is always better to be under-trained at the starting line of a race than it is to be sitting on the sidelines with an injury.

Note: I am a recreational runner and am not nor have I ever been an elite runner. All of these plans are developed for recreational runners. If high performance is your primary goal, seek the assistance of a qualified running coach. Running coaches can be found via Road Runners Club of America (http://www.rrca.org) or United States Track and Field (http://www.usatf.org.)

For each plan, there are different types of workouts. The plans are written using the terminology used by most training plans. If you are a new runner, don't be intimidated by the terminology. The concepts are pretty basic and are as follows:

- *Repeats:* A repeat is a very fast run (near-sprint) over a very short distance. When doing repeats you should not be able to hold a conversation. The purpose of a repeat is to build speed. Repeats are expressed as "A" x "B" where "A" is the number of times you run and "B" is the distance you run. Generally I rest one minute between each repeat. When running repeats barefoot it is important to never increase your pace more than 15 seconds per mile per week to help assure you remain injury-free. If you begin developing blisters you are going too fast for your current skill level.

- *Tempo Run:* A tempo run is slower than repeats, but still a fast run (10k pace.) Talking during a tempo run should be difficult, but possible. Most of my tempo run conversations consist of a series of undecipherable sounds. Tempo runs cover a longer distance than repeats with their purpose being to build speed over longer distances. When running tempo runs barefoot, it is important to never increase your pace more than 15 seconds per mile per week. Again, injury prevention is the goal.

- *Fartlek run:* As discussed in the Intermediate Barefoot Running section, a Fartlek run is a run of varying speeds and distances, and is a type of interval training. I vary the pace from a sprint to a walk and everywhere in between and like them because they add an element variety to a run. Same deal as repeats and tempo runs ... don't increase your pace too fast.

- *Long run:* The long run is a slow-paced run over a long distance at a pace that should be slow enough to allow you to easily hold a conversation. The purpose of the long run is to build endurance.

- *Hill repeats:* Hill repeats are simple—you run up and down a hill. I usually run up the hill with as much effort as I can muster. It is not uncommon for me to walk up the last few hills as fatigue sets in. This workout will build muscles, help develop hill running technique, and will improve speed. The hills I use are sand dunes, stairs, or a local Midwestern ski hill. Pretty much any kind of hill will work. Hill repeats are expressed as "Z" x hills where "Z" is the number of times you run up and down the hill. Generally, I rest one minute between each repeat.

- *Cross training:* Cross training includes any non-running activity. Some people use swimming, biking, yoga, martial arts, or playing an active sport (croquet, lawn darts and bowling don't count). I prefer a form of weight training known as high intensity interval training.

Many of the workouts will have a specific distance recommendation. There are a variety of methods used to track distances. An alternative to driving around in a car and using the odometer, try a good map website such as http://gmappedometer.com or Google Maps set on walking mode. Another way is to use a GPS watch. I've found it to be among my best running purchases.

5K Cheetah Plan

This plan is designed as a first step after finishing stage four of the transition plan earlier in this book. At this point you should be able to run at least two or three miles barefoot without pain. This plan will begin introducing speed to your workout.

The "Cheetah Plan" is designed with a 5K (3.1 mile) race in mind. At the conclusion of this plan you should be able to easily complete a 5K race barefoot or in minimalist shoes.

Week 1:
- Sunday – Rest day
- Monday – Tempo run: 1 mile
- Tuesday – Cross training day
- Wednesday – Intervals: 2 X 400 meters
- Thursday – Cross training
- Friday – Rest day
- Saturday – Long run: 2.25 miles

Week 2:
- Sunday – Rest day
- Monday – Tempo run: 1.25 miles
- Tuesday – Cross training day
- Wednesday – Hill repeats 2 x hills
- Thursday – Cross training
- Friday – Rest day
- Saturday – Long run: 2.5 miles

Week 3:
- Sunday – Rest day
- Monday – Tempo run: 1.5 miles
- Tuesday – Cross training day
- Wednesday – Fartlek run: 1.5 miles
- Thursday – Cross training
- Friday – Rest day
- Saturday – Long run: 2.75 miles

Week 4:
- Sunday – Rest day
- Monday – Tempo run: 1.75 miles
- Tuesday – Cross training day
- Wednesday – Intervals: 4 X 400 meters
- Thursday – Cross training
- Friday – Rest day
- Saturday – Long run: 3 miles

Week 5:
- Sunday – Rest day
- Monday – Tempo run: 2 miles
- Tuesday – Cross training day
- Wednesday – Hill Repeats: 4 x hills
- Thursday – Cross training
- Friday – Rest day
- Saturday – Long run: 3.25 miles

Week 6:
- Sunday – Rest day
- Monday – Tempo run: 2.25 miles
- Tuesday – Cross training day
- Wednesday – Fartlek run: 1.75 miles
- Thursday – Rest day (taper)
- Friday – Rest day (taper)
- Saturday – RACE DAY!

10K Pronghorn Plan

The "Pronghorn Plan" is intended to follow the "Cheetah Plan." It uses the same principles with added distances. If you are new to running, it would be best to go through the 5K plan first. This plan assumes you're comfortable running about three to four miles.

Week 1:
- Sunday – Rest day
- Monday – Tempo run: 1.5 miles
- Tuesday – Cross training day
- Wednesday – Hill Repeats: 3 x hills
- Thursday – Cross training
- Friday – Rest day
- Saturday – Long run: 3.5 miles

Week 2:
- Sunday – Rest day
- Monday – Fartlek run: 1.75 miles
- Tuesday – Cross training day
- Wednesday – Repeats: 3 x 400 meters
- Thursday – Cross training
- Friday – Rest day
- Saturday – Long run: 4 miles

Week 3:
- Sunday – Rest day
- Monday – Tempo run: 2 miles
- Tuesday – Cross training day
- Wednesday – Hill repeats: 4 x hills
- Thursday – Cross training
- Friday – Rest day
- Saturday – Long run: 4.5 miles

Week 4:
- Sunday – Rest day
- Monday – Fartlek run: 2.25 miles
- Tuesday – Cross training day
- Wednesday – Repeats: 4 x 400 meters
- Thursday – Cross training
- Friday – Rest day
- Saturday – Long run: 5 miles

Week 5:
- Sunday – Rest day
- Monday – Tempo run: 2.5 miles
- Tuesday – Cross training day
- Wednesday – Hill repeats: 5 x hills
- Thursday – Cross training
- Friday – Rest day
- Saturday – Long run: 5.5 miles

Week 6:
- Sunday – Rest day
- Monday – Fartlek run: 2.75 miles
- Tuesday – Cross training day
- Wednesday – Repeats: 5 x 400 meters
- Thursday – Cross training
- Friday – Rest day
- Saturday – Long run: 6 miles

Week 7:
- Sunday – Rest day
- Monday – Tempo run: 3 miles
- Tuesday – Cross training day
- Wednesday – Hill repeats: 6 x hills
- Thursday – Cross training
- Friday – Rest day
- Saturday – Long run: 6.5 miles

Week 8:
- Sunday – Rest day
- Monday – Fartlek run: 3.25 miles
- Tuesday – Cross training day
- Wednesday – Repeats: 6 x 400 meters
- Thursday – Rest day (taper)
- Friday – Rest day (taper)
- Saturday – RACE DAY!

Half Marathon Gazelle Plan

Moving up to the half-marathon distance (13.1 miles) requires the introduction of another training concept—rest weeks. When my training volume begins to increase, I will train hard for three weeks, and then schedule an easy week. The purpose is to allow your body to recover to some degree. This 12-week plan assumes you can run five or six miles comfortably.

Week 1:
- Sunday – Rest day
- Monday – Tempo run: 2.5 miles
- Tuesday – Cross training
- Wednesday – Hill repeats: 5 x hills
- Thursday – Cross training
- Friday – Fartlek run: 2.5 miles
- Saturday – Long run: 5 miles

Week 2:
- Sunday – Rest day
- Monday – Repeats: 6 x 400
- Tuesday – Cross training
- Wednesday – Tempo run: 2.75 miles
- Thursday – Cross training
- Friday – Hill repeats: 6 x hills
- Saturday – Long run: 6 miles

Week 3:
- Sunday – Rest day
- Monday – Fartlek run: 3 miles
- Tuesday – Repeats: 7 x 400
- Wednesday – Cross training
- Thursday – Tempo run: 3 miles
- Friday – Cross training
- Saturday – Long run: 7 miles

Week 4 (rest week):
- Sunday – Rest day
- Monday – Hill repeats: 3 x hills
- Tuesday – Cross training
- Wednesday – Fartlek run: 2 miles
- Thursday – Cross training
- Friday – Rest
- Saturday – Long run: 5 miles

Week 5:
- Sunday – Rest day
- Monday – Tempo run: 3.25 miles
- Tuesday – Hill repeats: 7 x hills
- Wednesday – Cross training
- Thursday – Fartlek run: 3.25 miles
- Friday – Cross training
- Saturday – Long run: 8 miles

Week 6:
- Sunday – Rest day
- Monday – Repeats: 8 x 400
- Tuesday – Cross training
- Wednesday – Tempo run: 3.5 miles
- Thursday – Cross training
- Friday – Hill repeats: 8 x hills
- Saturday – Long run: 9 miles

Week 7:
- Sunday – Rest day
- Monday – Fartlek run: 3.75 miles
- Tuesday – Cross training
- Wednesday – Repeats: 9 x 400
- Thursday – Cross training
- Friday – Tempo run: 3.75 miles
- Saturday – Long run: 10 miles

Week 8 (rest week):
- Sunday – Rest day
- Monday – Hill repeats: 6 x hills
- Tuesday – Cross training
- Wednesday – Fartlek run: 2 miles
- Thursday – Repeats: 6 X 400 meters
- Friday – Cross training
- Saturday – Long run: 8 miles

Week 9:
- Sunday – Rest day
- Monday – Tempo run: 4 miles
- Tuesday – Hill repeats: 11 x hills
- Wednesday – Cross training
- Thursday – Fartlek run: 4 miles
- Friday – Cross training
- Saturday – Long run: 8 miles

Week 10:
- Sunday – Rest day
- Monday – Repeats 12 x 400 meters
- Tuesday – Cross training
- Wednesday – Tempo run: 4.25 miles
- Thursday – Cross training
- Friday – Hill repeats: 12 x hills
- Saturday – Long run: 12 miles

Week 11:
- Sunday – Rest day
- Monday – Fartlek run: 4.5 miles
- Tuesday – Repeats: 12 x 400 meters
- Wednesday – Cross training
- Thursday – Tempo run: 4.5 miles
- Friday – Cross training
- Saturday – Long run: 13 miles

Week 12:
- Sunday – Rest day (taper)
- Monday – Fartlek run: 4.75 miles
- Tuesday – Rest day (taper)
- Wednesday – Repeats: 6 x 400 meters
- Thursday – Rest day (taper)
- Friday – Rest day (taper)
- Saturday – RACE DAY!

Marathon Hyena Plan

This 20-week plan will allow you to finish a marathon. When training for the marathon distance (26.2 miles/42.195K), the same basic principles apply. The addition of rest days allow your body to recuperate.

The four types of runs train your body for the rigors of running a marathon. The long run becomes increasingly important.

Use the long run to test various things like clothing, gear, pre-race meals, hydration strategies, etc. Like the half-marathon plan, this plan assumes you can comfortably run about five or six miles.

Week 1:
- Sunday – Rest
- Monday – Fartlek run: 2 miles
- Tuesday - Cross training
- Wednesday – Repeats: 6 x 400 meters
- Thursday – Tempo run: 2 miles
- Friday – Cross training
- Saturday – Long run: 5 miles

Week 2:
- Sunday – Rest
- Monday – Cross training
- Tuesday – Hill repeats: 7 x hills
- Wednesday – Fartlek runs: 2.25 miles
- Thursday – Cross training
- Friday – Repeats: 7 x 400
- Saturday – Long run: 6 miles

Week 3:
- Sunday – Rest
- Monday – Tempo run: 2 miles
- Tuesday – Cross training
- Wednesday – Hill repeats: 8 x hills
- Thursday – Rest
- Friday – Cross training
- Saturday – Long run: 7 miles

Week 4:
- Sunday – Rest
- Monday – Cross training
- Tuesday – Fartlek run: 2.75 miles
- Wednesday – Repeats: 9 x 400 meters
- Thursday – Cross training
- Friday – Tempo run: 2.75 miles
- Saturday – Long run: 8 miles

Week 5:
- Sunday – Rest
- Monday – Hill repeats: 10 x hills
- Tuesday – Cross training
- Wednesday – Fartlek run: 3 miles
- Thursday – Repeats: 10 x 400 meters
- Friday – Cross training
- Saturday – Long run: 9 miles

Week 6:
- Sunday – Rest
- Monday – Cross training
- Tuesday – Tempo run: 3.25 miles
- Wednesday – Hill repeats: 11 x hills
- Thursday – Cross training
- Friday – Fartlek run: 3.25 miles
- Saturday – Long run: 10 miles

Week 7 (rest week):
- Sunday – Rest
- Monday – Repeats: 6 x 400 meters
- Tuesday – rest
- Wednesday – Tempo run: 2 miles
- Thursday – Rest
- Friday – Cross training
- Saturday – Long run: 6 miles

Week 8:
- Sunday – Rest
- Monday – Cross training
- Tuesday – Hill repeats: 12 x hills
- Wednesday – Fartlek run: 3.5 miles
- Thursday – Cross training
- Friday – Repeats: 12 x 400
- Saturday – Long run: 11 miles

Week 9:
- Sunday – Rest
- Monday – Tempo Run: 3.75 miles
- Tuesday – Cross training
- Wednesday – Hill repeats: 13 x hills
- Thursday – Fartlek run: 3.75 miles
- Friday – Cross training
- Saturday – Long run: 13 miles

Week 10:
- Sunday – Rest
- Monday – Cross training
- Tuesday – Fatlek run: 4 miles
- Wednesday – Repeats: 14 x 400 meters
- Thursday – Cross training
- Friday – Tempo run: 4 miles
- Saturday – Long run: 15 miles

Week 11 (rest week):
- Sunday – Rest
- Monday – Hill repeats: 6 x hills
- Tuesday – Rest
- Wednesday – Fartlek run: 2 miles
- Thursday – Rest
- Friday – Cross training
- Saturday – Long run: 8 miles

Week 12:
- Sunday – Rest
- Monday – Cross training
- Tuesday – Repeats: 15 x 400 meters
- Wednesday – Tempo run: 4.25 meters
- Thursday – Cross training
- Friday – Hill repeats: 15 x hills
- Saturday – Long run: 17 miles

Week 13:
- Sunday – Rest
- Monday – Fartlek run: 4.5 miles
- Tuesday – Cross training
- Wednesday – Repeats: 16 x 400 meters
- Thursday – Tempo run: 4.5 miles
- Friday – Cross training
- Saturday – Long run: 19 miles

Week 14:
- Sunday – Rest
- Monday – Cross training
- Tuesday – Hill repeats: 16 x hills
- Wednesday – Fartlek run: 4.75 miles
- Thursday – Cross training
- Friday – Repeats: 16 x hills
- Saturday – Long run: 21 miles

Week 15 (rest week):
- Sunday – Rest
- Monday – Tempo run: 2 miles
- Tuesday – Rest
- Wednesday – Hill repeats: 6 x hills
- Thursday – Rest
- Friday – Cross training
- Saturday – Long run: 10 miles

Week 16:
- Sunday – Rest
- Monday – Cross training
- Tuesday – Fartlek run: 5 miles
- Wednesday – Repeats: 16 x 400 meters
- Thursday – Cross training
- Friday – Tempo run: 5 miles
- Saturday – Long run: 23 miles

Week 17:
- Sunday – Rest
- Monday – Hill repeats: 16 x hills
- Tuesday – Cross training
- Wednesday – Fartlek run: 5.25 miles
- Thursday – Repeats: 16 x hills
- Friday – Cross training
- Saturday – Long run: 25 miles

Week 18:
- Sunday – Rest
- Monday – Cross training
- Tuesday – Tempo run: 5.5 miles
- Wednesday – Hill repeats: 16 x hills
- Thursday – Cross training
- Friday – Fartlek run: 5.5 miles
- Saturday – Long run: 28 miles

Week 19:
- Sunday – Rest
- Monday – Repeats = 16 x 400 meters
- Tuesday – Cross training
- Wednesday – Tempo run: 5.75 miles
- Thursday – Hill repeats: 16 x hills
- Friday – Cross training
- Saturday – Long run: 15 miles

Week 20:
- Sunday – Rest
- Monday – Rest
- Tuesday – Repeats = 6 x 400 meters
- Wednesday – Rest
- Thursday – Rest
- Friday – Rest
- Saturday – RACE DAY!

Why Does My Foot Hurt Take Two ...
Can A Runner Relearn How to Run With Two Fused First Toe Joints?

The 2009 book *Born to Run* fascinated thousands of readers as author Christopher McDougall tried to answer the question of why his foot hurt. His discovery and recovery started with learning better running mechanics and was completed with his mission to the Copper Canyon to experience the Tarahumara. Along the way he concluded the modern running shoe designed with thick elevated heels was not the savior of the epidemic of running injuries, and in fact may be contributing. Current scientific research and the personal healing experiences of legions of runners doing Chi Running and running in shoes without heel elevation (and some even barefoot) is adding layers to the hard evidence and conceptual evidence both needed to change our running training and shoe design culture.

Now why would a Family Doctor be researching running injuries and experimenting with all types of running techniques and shoe designs in his free time? The answer lies in my quest to run completely pain free and with effortless efficient function with big toes that do not bend and in the more challenging quest to share the hard lessons learned with others wanting to keep moving for life.

I have been a runner since age 13 and ran competitively at University of Virginia in the mid 80's. As an often injured runner, my interest in medicine was sparked after experiencing our team physician Dr. Danial Kulund of Charlottesville trying some seemingly bizarre at the time and innovative approaches to running injuries. He was the first to have people run in the pool and built softer lightweight orthotics in his toaster oven. It seemed like there must be better ways to treat these maladies and Dr. Kulund blazed his own path. Dr. Kulund was one of the first to encourage water running for training and rehab and had a deep hot-tub-sized pool in his office with a tether. He gave elite and recreational runners rebirth by his methods. Runners train in water now not just as injury rehab, but for prevention and supplemental training. Twenty years into my medical career I am reviving the passion I felt at that time by working with innovators in running technique, functional strength, safer aerobic conditioning, and foot wear design.

Dr. George Sheehan was another pioneer and his ideas were also way ahead of his time. I read *Running and Being* in high school and did not really understand a lot of what he was talking about then ... but now I do. Holism, prevention, understanding movement and the root causes of injury—that is the holy grail of running pain-free for life.

"If athletes were given less care and more thought, the doctors might come up with some original ideas on why illness persists, why injury doesn't clear up. If more non-physicians could be induced to lend their ideas and talents, we might see a completely new approach to sports medicine." —Dr. George Sheehan 1975

A modern innovator applying these innovative and integrated principles is Jay Dicharry at The University of Virginia Speed Clinic. His inquisitiveness and pursuit of new methods gave me the opportunity to present ChiRunning research at the 2008 and 2009 UVA Running Medicine Conference and our community running event, Freedom's Run, as a model for community engagement at the 2010 Conference. Jay connects form, function, performance, and injury prevention and empowers those he sees with insight, cues, and detailed instruction to self correction. He is producing the needed research to prove the principles that "Natural Running" speaks of.

We live in a sportsmedicine world now where running injuries are still treated with rest, ice, new and bulkier shoes, stretching, MRI's, other fancy tests, and various other devices. Despite all this care, of which there is little to no evidence base, we are still getting injured at the same high rates. Runners are becoming former runners not by choice, but out of suggestion from the health care field as the answer to their body's discomforts.

I've been through the pain cycles too in younger years. Frequently hurt, I managed sub 2:25 marathons with the usual busy school and job commitments of a physician. I discovered in 2000, after years of progressive pain in my feet, that severe arthritis had engulfed both my large toe joints. The technical term is hallux rigidus and causes are many including: pushing off too hard on a dorsiflexed first toe repetitively, running and walking in shoes with a heel placing unnatural forces on the toe joints, and other genetic and/or biomechanical deficits. Women suffer damaging arthritis in this joint 4 to 5 times the rate of men. One can reason that a large contributor may be elevating the heel and placing unnatural forces to this joint as we walk and stand all day.

I decided to have bone resections for the arthritis changes in both great toe MTP joints (joint where toe attaches to foot). I could not dorsiflex (bend up) either great toe MTP joints due to the degenerative changes. The surgery relieved some of the pain but the joint was still essentially fused straight. I thought my days of running pain-free were done....this was the orthopedic message. Perhaps take up another activity? None were as convenient and relaxing as running.

After taking a few post operative months off in early 2000, I was set on trying to retool how I ran with only one goal—getting out and enjoying myself. I lived off a wooded park in Denver where everyone ran, Washington Park. It had a crush surface 2.5 mile loop which one never tires of.

I studied what was written on running methods and found that some concepts made sense for impact reduction and optimizing forces and momentum. Common themes were shorter stride and quicker cadence, not overstriding and braking, a slight forward lean, and landing more midfoot under one's center of mass. I also tried to figure out how the Kenyans ran ... they had no shoes so had to have low impact styles. I trained "easy" by the method made popular by Phil Maffetone and used by Priscilla Welch and Mark Allen. I incorporated a full understanding of the Lydiard method also.

This method focuses on becoming completely efficient at one's pure aerobic heart rate. This is the level where fat utilization is the primary fuel source. It builds the aerobic system to its maximal potential. The runner becomes efficient in form and metabolism, building millions of capillary beds and the mitochondria to produce aerobic energy at a set low heart rate. With weeks of patience the pace drops and drops with the same low heart rate. The runner morphs from a pure gas car (glucose as fuel) to an efficient hybrid, using electric (fat) as primary fuel and turning on the gas when you need it.

http://www.markallenonline.com/heartrate.asp

Surprisingly with this "easy" running and study of some technique, I rebounded to run a 2:28 at 2000 Marine Corps Marathon after only 4 months back to running and no more than 60 miles per week. I also recovered easier than ever before.

I could visualize the "land with bent knees" and "under center of mass" that the methods were describing. I understood what not to do ... do not land on the heels, but did not really get what to do. What areas did one focus on to generate movement? How could I explain this simply to a patient or runner?

I coached "Team in Training" in Denver and was the regional doc there. I shared these principles of low impact and aerobic-only training with a group that often became hurt unless guided correctly.

I continued to have successful marathons but still had occasional breakdowns in later miles. Ran a 2:39 at the 2005 Marine Corps which was not really satisfying, but figured I was getting older and busier with life (kids now).

In December 2005 there was an article in the Sunday Washington Post on ChiRunning. The short article was intriguing and led me to buy the book. After the first read and a little practice, I realized what I was missing in trying to find and teach efficient injury-free running—draw the power from the core and "lift the legs" while off-loading the feet. This was a method I could visualize completely. But more importantly as a physician I knew this was a teachable method for the masses of recreational runners who were often injured while trying to run more comfortably and were afraid to, or told not to, run anymore.

I also studied foot anatomy as related to stance and gait. When a heel is elevated the arch of the foot destabilizes and a domino effect of compensations occur. When a heel is elevated the large toe cannot stabilize the arch in the designed way and the 5th metatarsal, another key stability structure, is lifted off the ground.

Through application of these principles, I have continued to run marathons in under 2:35. Finished 2:34 In the 2010 Boston Marathon to make it 22 of last 24 years with a time under this mark (missed during my medical intern year and in 2009 when I ran 2:37). In my 40th year I won the Air Force Marathon outright in 2:31, have won 2 Master's Division Marine Corps Marathons, and 3 successful 50-milers at the highly competitive JFK 50-Mile Run (16th place in 2007 and 11th place and first Master in 2008, and 21st place in 2010). Could not imagine lining up for the ultra distances without the secret weapon of ChiRunning in the tool kit. I am running now in a magical feeling by putting my foot down, leaning slightly in controlled fall, and just picking my foot off the ground. No stress, bending, or pain in the large toe joint.

As a physician seeking to find new, innovative ways to treat injury, the Chi Running method cried out for study. The first step was surveying the users for results and comments. In late 2007 Danny Dreyer sent 25,000 email surveys with a 10% response. This is good in the world of survey research. The results showed dramatic decreases of injury and effort, and a quick learning curve. The part which really convinced me to continue to validate this method was the over 1000 comments, many of which were nothing short of life-changing testimonials to ChiRunning. We followed this with a small prospective pilot study in 2008 and even in a small group with a brief intervention found that folks can learn form and reduce effort. My wife is a researcher and she told me once, "The plural of anecdote is not fact." So we are continuing to pursue studies for more proof of principle.

Now that I'd discovered better movement and was trying to answer if others could do the same, the natural evolution was the intriguing question of whether footwear matters. At the time I was running for Brooks and had great conversations with designer Trip Allen. Trip also believed that shoes with heels were an impediment to better mechanics and had prototype designs with no heel lift. He advised me to cut off the heel part of my Brooks Burn—his original design had no heel lift. This shoe felt great and I completed marathons and 2 JFK 50-Mile runs in the shoe with the hack-sawed heel. Jay Dicharry encourages the use of a rigid turf toe plate under the large toe joint for protection. This helped the toe but I lost some of the natural feel for the road and trail.

The beauty of focusing on form is that we all continue to improve, sometimes in small steps and often in leaps. None of us are close to perfect. We dream of one day running on water. Form improvements and complementary footwear have given me running longevity, made it easier and painless, and has given me confidence I can run forever into the retirement home.

A concluding statement from the Exercise Physiology gurus at the Science of Sport (http://www.sportscientists.com/2010_03_01_archive.html) ties all this together. On making the observation that "natural" running form may now indeed be landing on the heels, perhaps by the influence of soft-cushioned heels, they state:

" ... I believe the natural way to run is the unadjusted one, but the best way to run is the modified natural form. And of course, equipment will influence this."

"Natural Running" is applied physics and biomechanics that you can apply to your benefit. No pain ... no gain—a thing of the past. No pain....thank you—the natural way.

Mark Cucuzzella MD, FAAFP
Associate Professor of Family Medicine West Virginia University
Lt. Col. US Air Force Reserves
Race Director Freedom's Run—An Event for Health and Heritage

Cross Training

The Barefoot Workout

"Everyone is an athlete. The only difference is that some of us are in training, and some are not." —George Sheehan

The workout suggested in this section is just one of many workouts that will have a positive impact on your running. Any cross training is beneficial with some runners electing to ride a bike, swim, participate in yoga or Pilates, or a myriad of other activities. The general idea is to engage your body in different movements which will result in maintaining and strengthening those body parts that are not engaged while running. This will help promote a resiliency to injury, increase recovery time, and ultimately increase overall running performance.

Here are the guiding principles that guide *The Barefoot Workout*:

High intensity workouts produce better results.

Workouts should leave you feeling physically exhausted and covered in sweat. This is not a "country club" workout.

**All exercises should promote strength
across multiple planes.**

Most exercises require coordination and balance, thus work, and build all the stabilizer muscles throughout your body. This also works your core muscles which are critical to running. For myself, I avoid most exercises that allow only a single plane of motion (Nautilus machines, etc.)

Variety is essential.

On any given week I may do 20-60 *different* exercises. This assures ALL muscle groups are used. Based on my experiences, this is the best possible weight training method for running.

Many of my exercises and theories about weight training were developed based on the teachings of Crossfit® (http://crossfit.com) and Crossfit Endurance® (http://crossfitendurance.

com). I highly recommend both programs to all runners. A good friend, Pete Kemme, was also instrumental in the development of this program. His creative inspiration and desire for masochistic workouts fueled my own desire to design The Barefoot Workout. Finally, Dean Jewett of Jewett Strength and Conditioning (http://www.jewettstrength.com) helped influence the development of this workout.

The Barefoot Workout Format

There are five different "formats" I use for my cross training workout. Each of the formats is designed around the principles stated above and provide variety which will keep the workouts fresh and entertaining.

When doing this workout, I suggest randomly picking a method by placing the names in a hat. Once chosen, leave that format out until all formats have been chosen.

For each workout format, you will be asked to choose a number of exercises from three groups which are listed in the next section, along with a brief description of each exercise.

Tabata Format: The Tabata protocol was developed by Izumi Tabata, a Japanese researcher. His protocol was originally used to train skaters. I adopted the format because it presents an interesting challenge that builds strength and cardiovascular endurance.

The format is simple: Do an exercise for 30 seconds, then rest for 20 seconds. Repeat this cycle eight times. The original Tabata research was based on 20/10 second intervals, but I've had better results with the 30/20 intervals.

When doing the "Tabata workout" pick two exercises from the first group, two from the second group, and one from the third. Do these five exercises in any order.

Here's a sample of the Tabata format:

Exercise #1 is pull-ups. Start a timer or watch. Do as many pull-ups as you can in 30 seconds. When the 30 seconds expires, rest for 20 seconds. When the resting time ends, do as many pull-ups as possible in 30 seconds, then rest for 20 seconds. Repeat this cycle eight times. After the eighth cycle, rest for one minute. After the one minute rest period, move on to exercise #2. Repeat this process until all five exercises are completed.

Advanced Tabata workout: Add more exercises.

Interval Format: The interval format introduces the element of running mixed with high intensity exercise intervals. This format requires a place to safely run or a treadmill.

The basic idea is simple. You will do an exercise for two minutes, and then run a predetermined distance. The distance can vary by experience, but I find 400 meters to be sufficient.

Choose two exercises from the first group, two exercises from the second group, and one exercise from the third.

Here's a sample of the interval format:

Exercise #1 is wall ball. Start a timer or watch. Do as many wall ball throws as you can in two minutes. At the end of two minutes, run the predetermined distance. When you return, take a one minute break. At the end of the one minute break, proceed to exercise #2. Continue this cycle until you complete all five exercises.

Advanced interval format: Add more exercises.

Crossfit's© "Fight Gone Bad" Format: This format is one of the Crossfit Workouts of the Day©. For this format, you will choose two exercises from the first group, two from the second group, and one from the third.

When you begin, you will do the five exercises for one minute each with no rest period. At the conclusion of the five minute exercise period, you will rest for one minute. Then repeat the exercise cycle. This exercise/rest cycle will be repeated three times.

Here is a sample of the Fight Gone Bad format:
• Sumo deadlift high pull
• Wall sit
• Thrusters

- Burpees
- Walking lunges

Start a timer or watch. Begin by doing sumo deadlift high pull for one minute. Immediately switch to a wall sit. Switch to thrusters after one minute. When a minute passes, move on to burpees. You will finish with walking lunges. After lunges, rest for one minute. Repeat this cycle two more times.

Advanced Fight Gone Bad format: Add more sets. Do four or five cycles of the five exercises.

Mount Everest Format: This format will appear to be very easy, but becomes impossibly difficult. That is the reason I love it. For this exercise, you will need a clock, timer, or some other device to track time.

Pick one exercise except wall sits or jump rope. When time begins, do one repetition of the exercise during the first minute. During the second minute, do two repetitions. For the third minute, do three repetitions. The object is to go as long as possible while maintaining this pattern.

Advanced Mount Everest format: After the first exercise, do the same format with an exercise from a different group.

Sweat Poker Format: This format is added for the gamblers out there. It really has nothing to do with poker other than the use of playing cards.

Choose four exercises; one from each group and a fourth of your choosing. Like the Mount Everest format, avoid the wall sit and jump rope exercises.

Assign one suit to each exercise. For example:
- Hearts = Hindu pushups
- Spades = Jumping scissors
- Diamonds = Box jumps
- Clubs = Tuck jumps

Each numerical value on individual cards represents the number of repetitions you will do. The suit will determine the exercise. For example, when you turn up the seven of clubs, do seven tuck jumps. All numerical cards are face value. Jacks are worth 11, queens are worth 12, kings worth 13, and aces are worth 14.

Shuffle the deck of playing cards. When ready, turn the first card over. Do the prescribed number of repetitions. Immediately turn over the next card and do that prescribed number of repetitions.

Warning: this workout is very difficult. It may be advantageous to use a partial deck in the beginning.

Advanced Sweat Poker format: Use multiple decks.

Avoid an Overuse Injury

If all you do is run barefoot-style, you're probably going to suffer an overuse injury. You also need to exercise, walk and, ideally, hike in your bare feet or in Vibrams, to allow your feet and legs to get stronger. Feet need time to develop from the state of atrophy they've achieved in your shoes.

Tucker Goodrich
Senior Member,
Barefoot Ted's Google Group

The Exercises

Each of the exercises below was chosen because each one accomplishes specific goals related to balanced cross training. As a runner, it is important to work muscle groups that compliment running motions. If we rely on running alone, muscle imbalances develop which leads to injury.

Try to avoid repeating an exercise until all exercises have been completed. This will help assure a high degree of variability, which will help assure no muscle groups are left unchallenged.

Also, most exercises require minimal equipment. What kind of instructor would I be if I don't stick to the minimalist theme?

Group One

Sumo deadlift high pull: This exercise requires either a barbell or dumbbell.

Hindu pushups

Pull-ups: This exercise requires a pullup bar.

One-handed clean and press: This exercise requires either a barbell or dumbbell.

Wall ball: This exercise requires a medicine ball.

Burpees

Group Two

Walking Lunges

Jumping Scissors

Tuck Jump

Wall sit

Knee taps

Jump rope: This exercise requires a jump rope.

Group Three

Turkish getups: This exercise requires a dumbbell or barbell.

Burpee pull-ups: This exercise requires a pullup bar.

Thrusters: This exercise requires a pullup bar.

Medicine ball get-ups: This exercise requires a medicine ball.

Frog jumps with walkout and pushup

Box jumps: This exercise requires a plyometric platform (or any other stable object that can be used to jump on).

The Body God Intended Us to Use

Some call me crazy. Others just find what I do a little strange, simply because I do not work out in a traditional manner. I want to discuss what it is that I do, why it is important to anybody that wants to have a healthy life, what are the specifics of a workout, and finally I will give some guidance on how to take it up a notch so you too can be "crazy."

There are many different ways to exercise or to "get into shape." First, I want to talk about what I call functional fitness. One of the main proponents of this concept is Crossfit, which has created a user-friendly, access to all, enterprise that has been quite successful. Anybody can access their website and check out the Workout of the Day (WOD). In fact, a great deal of the foundation for the workout program I use is based upon the principles shared by Crossfit. A similar, although much more closed off and elite, version is Gym Jones. Gym Jones is literally an exclusive gym out in Utah, and they are famous for sculpting the bodies of the actors for the movie, *300*.

What I have learned from Crossfit, Gym Jones, Ross Training, and others is the concept of functional strength, but how I achieve that differs in some areas. I rarely time my workouts, unlike Crossfit, as I am not worried about creating a competitive and energetic atmosphere in a gym. I personally feel that the recommendation from the American Heart Association to have my heart rate increased for a period of thirty to forty minutes is something not to be ignored. Seriously, how can you argue with those folks. Functional strength to me means that I can shovel my driveway without being crippled the next day. It means that I can haul a 4X8 sheet of 1/2 inch OSB board across my yard and hold it up while I nail it in place without having my back spasm. It means that as I age, I can still pick up my children, and eventually grandchildren, without moaning and groaning. Functional strength means that I can perform the functions necessary in life the way God intended me to. Forget OSHA requirements not to use your back and lift solely with your legs. God gave us the gluteus maximus and huge muscles on our backs. Build them! Use them!

Our bodies are meant to work as a whole. We need to train our muscles to work together, and that takes practice, especially if you have been isolating muscles your whole life. In order for muscles to work together, you brain needs to create the neural connections. I'm simplifying things here, but basically you need to train your brain to activate all the muscles--not just the big ones--at the same time, in order to accomplish a task such as carrying a couch up from the basement. You don't curl the couch. You don't bench press the couch. You carry it awkwardly, while one foot is on a higher step and your wife is yelling at you not to bump into the wall, which is impossible since you are turning the corner and have to all of a sudden adjust the entire angle of the couch to fit through. That is functional strength. That is your body working the way it is meant to.

What I want to do is to change the way most people think about exercising. Most people will either do some weight lifting and/or some cardio. You know, "today I'm working my chest and biceps while tomorrow I'm doing some cardio." This is what I want you to say: "Today I am doing something fun." It will work your chest. It will work your biceps. It will be cardiovascular in nature, but it will also activate your core, force your muscles to work together, work all your muscles in your body--and for us crazy ones--it will fatigue all your muscles so that in the end you are curled up on the floor in the fetal position. Another change in thought is that you have to let go the idea of "being big." Huge pectorals and biceps are only good for turning heads at the beach. Yes, you do have strength, but it is only two dimensional. I suppose if a log were to fall on you while you are laying flat on your back, you could push it up. Of course when you try to throw it off to the side, you will probably pop a rib out of place since none of those muscles around your core have been used in years. But don't worry about not being big. Having all those little tiny muscles showing when you take your shirt off will still turn some heads at the beach. And you don't even have to flex to show off your muscles! That is because they are more dense and not just temporarily "puffed up."

There are many different routine styles to choose from to create your workouts. Honestly, your imagination is the only limit here. Many of my workouts involve roughly three routines. My first routine is sometimes slower paced, but involves more strength such as dead lifts and one arm barbell presses. Throw in something like push-ups at the end, repeat two or three times, and you have a nice little circuit. The second routine in the workout will be the main dish, and the final routine is where I try to finish myself off with total muscle fatigue. Another style would be to do 400 reps of various exercises, such as 25 burpees, 20 split squat jumps, 20 one arm/one leg dumbbell clean and press, etc. Some days I just take a heavy medicine ball and head into a stairwell for forty minutes. Believe me there are tons of things to do alone in a stairwell with a medicine ball, and none of them are illegal!

If you haven't noticed already, I like using one arm and/or one leg. That is an easy way to turn an ordinary two dimensional exercise into a three dimensional core building exercise. Not to mention it is fun to see the looks you get from the mainstream exercisers in your gym when your barbell is sticking out completely to one side since you are holding it on the extreme far end as opposed to in the middle. Another good way to change an exercise is to do it on the physioball, such as one arm dumbbell curl and press while you are kneeling on the ball. I also use a lot of body weight exercises such as burpees, different kinds of push-ups, and pull ups. Again the goal is not to "get bigger," but to be stronger. I always have 155 pounds of weight to use whenever I want to thanks to my own bodyweight. If you don't own a kettlebell, buy one. If you don't have medicine balls, buy them (or make them out of a basketball and sand). I have a 20 pound sand-filled basketball I named Carl. By the way, you get to name your homemade equipment, as well as any kettlebell (since those are expensive).

The key to any workout routine is that is works your whole body, keeps your heart rate up for 30 to 40 minutes, activates your core, and does not isolate muscles. The final, and most important thing to remember, is to have fun and do as many weird things you can think of. I usually don't do the same workout for months, as I create new ones all the time.

You want to know how to be crazy? Make sure you keep your pace up, and therefore your heart rate, while trying exciting exercises such as the Turkish get-up, and to work yourself into complete muscle fatigue. I don't recommend the latter for beginners or those with certain medical conditions. That is merely for us crazy folk (and those training for MMA fights). That brings me to a final note. It is good to have a goal. Maybe you want to enhance your gymnastic abilities because it is just cool. Or maybe you are training for soccer season. Or maybe you want to reduce your back pain. Or maybe you want to run the Warrior Dash. Whatever your goal, it can help focus you when you create your workouts and motivate you during them. Above all, enjoy using your body the way God intended.

Pete Kemme   http://kemmefitness.com

My Adventures

Hallucination 100 Race Report

The following is the race report I wrote after completing the Hallucination 100 Mile Run, part of the Woodstock Running Festival in Pinckney, Michigan in September of 2009.

I decided to add this adventure as it was the culmination of my barefoot running efforts and I would not have been able to make this journey if it were not for the inspiring words from my fellow ultrarunners in other race reports. These race reports can be a wealth of information. I encourage every runner to share their thoughts, experiences, and general adventures by writing their own race reports for their more memorable races.

The Seed is Planted

The year was 2004. We were watching the Janet Jackson Super Bowl at our friends' house. Doug, an old work friend of Shelly's, mentioned running the local 25K road race. I was amazed. Who would run 15.5 miles?!? That brought up the insanity of running a marathon and those crazy people who run 26.2 miles! At that point the furthest I had run was a four mile adventure while in high school. Then Doug uttered words that would haunt me for years, "There are even longer races called ultramarathons and some are one hundred miles long!"

Moments later, the now-famous wardrobe malfunction occurred. I missed it because I was entranced by this idea that people would run 100 miles at one time. Little did I know that wintery day in 2004 would change my life. The following spring, Shelly and I started running regularly. The thought of ultramarathons brewed in the back of my mind that entire year prompting me to do some research. The more I discovered, the more intrigued I became. That following year, Shelly and I decided to enter a local 15K. It led me to my first attempt at training for a 50-mile ultramarathon scheduled for September.

I trained hard all summer but repeated injuries derailed my mileage making me settle for the marathon version of that race. During that marathon I managed to finish but suffered with pain. Then I ran another marathon a few weeks later.

Then in 2006, I decided to run a 50-miler. That spring, my father passed away due to a major heart attack—a lifetime of smoking ultimately led to his death. His death had a profound impact on me. My second child was born a week after he died, and I did not want my children to lose their father like I had. My quest to complete an ultramarathon became a near-obsessive quest to ensure my health.

Doug's words about ultramarathons continued to echo in my head—"Some are one hundred miles long." To reach my goal, I knew I would have to overcome the injury bug. My exhaustive research led to barefoot running, which I adapted in earnest. During that first year there were many trials and tribulations as I made about every mistake a new barefoot runner could make. Still, I seemed to avoid major injuries.

That fall I ran and finished my first 50-mile race, the North Country Trail Run. Running through the forest alone was an incredibly emotional experience reminding me of the many days spent hunting with my dad. I felt a powerful connection to the wilderness which made the race especially emotional. I knew I wasn't ready for the 100-miler yet, so instead I ran the 50-miler again in 2007. Once again, I finished without major problems and decided I would be ready to run the 100-miler the next time.

In 2008, I entered and ran the Burning River 100-mile race in Northeast Ohio. However I made many stupid mistakes, hit a serious wall, and ultimately gave up and walked my way to being pulled from the course at about mile 65. It was a devastating blow to my confidence because it was the first time I had really tried to do something and failed miserably. That raised serious doubts about my ability to finish a 100-miler. Maybe I just didn't have what it takes.

Hallucination

As 2009 rolled around, I was undecided about attempting another 100-miler. Some major personal issues resulted in incredible self-growth through the spring and early summer. At some point during this time I reevaluated my goals as a runner. I had this obsessive drive to run 100 miles, but *why?*

I concluded I was seeking the adulation that comes with doing something others cannot fathom and slowly began to realize my quest had to be more about my own spiritual growth and not about the outside world. Finishing a 100-miler became the final act in my transformation from being a troubled, broken person if I was to be the person I wished to become.

Scouring the ultra schedules looking for a race that would match my available time frame—as luck would have it—I discovered a brand-new event only two hours from my house. The Woodstock Running Festival featured a few short races, a half-marathon, a marathon, a 50K, a 50-miler, and a 100-miler called The Hallucination 100! I liked the sound of that!

I immediately began working on a training schedule. My goal was to correct the mistakes I had made the previous year at Burning River. Most importantly, my wife was unbelievably supportive agreeing to make the trip and crew for me. This was the single best motivator I could have received. I also solicited additional help from some other friends to help me complete my journey.

As for training, I knew I needed more miles. To do this I ran more, including more night runs. This allowed me to become an expert at running trails at night. I also had to work on my eating during the race and experimented with every food imaginable before settling on ice cream, pancakes, and hot dogs. In addition, I decreased my weightlifting routine, increased my mileage, and lost some more weight. That resulted in me running the Burning River 100-miler at about 184 pounds. Then, for Hallucination, I was down to around 177 pounds. Beyond that I tweaked a few other things, including simplifying my crew plans and bringing more socks to change into. I vowed to be ready.

The Crew

Before I knew it, race weekend was here and our crew was set to meet up. The crew consisted of:

Shelly Robillard—My wife and mother to our three wonderful children. Shelly is a runner, but had just given birth five months earlier. She assumed the role of official crew chief.

Jason Saint Amour—My friend from elementary school who, as noted earlier, ran barefoot with me during high school. Jason started running after crewing for me the previous year and went on to train for the half-marathon at Woodstock, but hurt his ankle the Sunday before.

Mark Robillard—My running friend that is also my unofficial older brother. He is an experienced trail runner and finished a trail marathon the previous week. Mark was our "picture man."

Stuart Peterson—A friend of Mark's who I met briefly beforehand. He was known as "RV Man" for the 32 foot RV he brought that acted as our base of operations.

Michael Helton—A friend from the *Runner's World* Barefoot Forum (he's known as Notleh there). I had never met Michael in person prior to the Friday before the race, but I knew he ran barefoot, had a great sense of humor, drank beer, and would have no problem doing whatever it took to get me to the finish line.

Rich Elliott—Technically not part of the crew, but he made the trip with us. He was attempting to run the 50-miler with training that consisted of a 5K road race three weeks earlier.

The race was to be run in Pinckney, Michigan, on Saturday morning at 6 a.m. To prepare, I took Friday off to pack, shop for groceries, and pick up a few running supplies. Around ten thirty, I picked Shelly up from the school where we teach and ran to McDonald's to grab a quick bite to eat. Quarter-Pounders are a favorite pre-race food of mine.

We picked up Rich and headed to Jason's house, which was near the race location. During the two hour ride I was a nervous wreck, sweating profusely and even shaking a bit. I felt like a gamer emerging from his mother's basement for his first date. That was how nervous I was. Luckily, by the time we arrived at Jason's I calmed down and was able to unload our gear and talk a bit before heading to the race site where we would be meeting Michael.

Jason drove his Honda Element with me riding shotgun and Rich in the back seat with Shelly. While I pulled out my phone to get directions, Jason fired up his GPS. We later discovered both of us had entered different destinations. Jason followed his GPS directions when, at some point, I realized we were heading in the wrong direction. After much confusion we managed to reach the race site. Luckily, we were still early. Because Michael wouldn't be arriving for at least another hour, we decided to find a bar, grab a bite to eat and have a few beers.

Eventually we ended up at the Dexter Bar, a small pub in the equally-small town of Dexter. Going on the theory that carb-loading is good and beer has carbs, I drank two tall Killian's to wash down our order of nachos.

After about an hour or two, Michael showed up. We talked awhile to get acquainted, had another beer, and then headed back to Jason's house. We hung out there for a little while, got hungry, and then headed to the Fenton House restaurant for pizza and breadsticks with parmesan dip where Mark and Stuart joined us. As we talked about the race logistics it occurred to me we really hadn't done much planning. Stuart eased the building anxiety by asking Michael for his uneaten pizza crust that was sitting on his plate, thus displaying his easy going personality that would pay dividends later when he took over pacing me at six o'clock Sunday morning.

From the restaurant we walked the two blocks back to Jason's house, stopping along the way to check out Stuart's massive RV parked behind the restaurant. I had expected something more modest on the order of a large van. We got back to Jason's house, had a beer, and then crashed around ten o'clock. Exhausted, I fell asleep almost immediately.

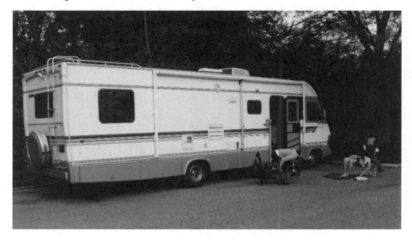

Race Morning

Three a.m. came early. I needed time to go through my routine, but it was tough. Pulling on some clothes, I walked around Jason's yard to loosen up. When I returned to the house, Jason was awake so we headed out to get some coffee. Due to superstitions, Jason wanted McDonald's while I needed Speedway gas station coffee.

At McDonald's the coffee machine was broken so we decided to return after getting my coffee from Speedway. Once we had our coffee we headed back to Jason's house where I ate my requisite cream cheese coffee cake and drank a 24-ounce cappuccino. After jumping in the shower, dressing and strapping on my Vibram KSOs, we packed the car and headed out. I was amazingly calm during the trip to the race considering how much a nervous wreck I was the day before. It was during this ride that Rich threw out his now-famous, "anyone can run fifty miles if they train for it" quote which helped calm my nerves. The rest of the trip was uneventful as Shelly and I reviewed our race and aid station strategy.

Once at the start/finish line, we met up with Michael, Mark, and Stuart. The air was a strange combination of cool and humid as if it were about to rain. I thought my choice of attire was well-planned, however my crew couldn't resist teasing me about the GAP sweatshirt I was wearing, which was a good-luck charm. Every other runner and most of their pacers and crew were wearing official running attire while my clothes  appeared to be pulled from the "lost and found." Perhaps I'm not the snazziest dresser.

We milled about, talked to a few other runners, and then got the call to line up. Rich and I would be starting together, and decided to start near the back of the pack next to a local guy who regularly trained on the trails. While he gave us some good information about the terrain, in my nervousness I forgot everything within seconds. After a few minutes, and some directions from the race director, we were given the signal to start. We slogged through the timing gate, and then headed out over the damp grass. Let the adventure begin!

We passed a few people before the trail head, where we were funneled into a single file line. Rich fell in behind me with maybe eight or ten people behind us. Almost immediately a light rain began. We had emergency rain ponchos, but I decided not to use mine right away.

The course started with a boardwalk over a swampy area, then a root-filled rocky hill followed by another and another—a pattern that would repeat itself throughout the race.

We did get a quick reprieve from the rockiness when going through the "Crooked Lake Commune" campground where other runners and crew cheered us enthusiastically while awaiting later race starts. It was a cool feeling.

A soon as we exited the campground, it began to pour. My precious GAP sweatshirt was absorbing water, but the other two layers kept me warm. Then, almost as soon as it began, it stopped. That would be the extent of the rain for the remainder of the race.

The first leg was slow—about half of the time was spent walking as the trail was not conducive to passing at this point. I relaxed and just focused on warming up. The earlier rain had left the downhill sections especially slippery with some runners slipping and sliding repeatedly. The smooth soles of the Vibrams provided poor traction, but I was able to avoid unnecessary slipping and falling because of good form. There's a definite advantage to running with your weight under your center of gravity.

After about 45 minutes or so, we hit the first aid station. It was a zoo with nearly every runner and their corresponding crews fighting for supplies. My crew was eagerly awaiting our arrival, but there was considerable confusion as each member tried to accomplish the tasks I had given them. I swapped the water bottle from my handheld for a full bottle and guzzled about two cups of a Ben and Jerry's Cookies and Cream/milk concoction. I decided to save the clothes and sock change until the next aid station. Rich refilled his water bottle, and then we were off. While the stop took a bit longer than planned, the crew learned and adjusted accordingly.

The second leg started with rugged terrain featuring lots of hills and roots. Rich was still behind me, but starting to look a bit tired based on my pace. I was running at about a 20 hour pace at the 12-mile point. The crowd thinned out a bit, but I didn't do too much passing. I took my last Succeed electrolyte tablet as the sun was beginning to rise.

I was starting to get warm, so it was a relief to get to the second aid station where I ditched the sweatshirt and hat, swapped my water bottle, and replaced my stash of electrolytes. Sitting on a chair, I pulled off my socks. The Injinjis were pretty wet but my feet looked good. I doused them with powder, put on fresh socks, and slipped into the Vibrams. The last task was to reapply Sportslick lube to my groin/thigh area. The tube was freezing cold and hard as a rock but I managed to coax some out, handed the tube back to Jason, and asked him to keep it warm. Rich and I left this aid station in pretty good time. It seemed as if the crew was a little more organized.

The next section was about two and a half miles. I didn't know it at the time, but crew access here was tough. During this leg we passed a few runners though Rich seemed to be slowing down a little just as I was warming up. I made the decision to start pulling away knowing that building a good time-padding now would be critical for the second half of the race. My pre-race strategy called for as much running as possible for as long as possible.

In Burning River, I tried using a run/walk ratio of four to one which ultimately put me too close to the cutoff time. This time I used a race strategy given to me by Jeremiah Cataldo, an ultrarunning friend who had recently finished his first 100-miler—the Mohican. His strategy was simple: run as long as you can, only walk the up hills.

This next section was relatively smooth with fewer rolling hills as I settled into a comfortable pace. Soon there were several runners between Rich and myself. When I arrived at the next aid station my crew was nowhere to be found. Since it was a short leg, it wasn't an issue. I refilled my bottle with a mixture of Gatorade and water, grabbed a Gu for the trail, and headed out.

The fourth section started out silky smooth but got rough quickly. During this leg I talked with a few runners including a guy who had fallen multiple times. Even though this was his first 50-miler, he was looking strong despite being covered in mud.

I also met up with a man who was checking the ribbons used to mark the course. We talked for a few miles before he turned back. He also worked the course for Dances with Dirt, a notoriously difficult race held in the same area. I was unaware Dances with Dirt used the same course. Based on the horror stories I'd heard about that race, this new revelation worried me.

I also encountered what would come to be my nemesis throughout the daytime hours—mountain bikers! While the vast majority of the bikers I encountered were considerate and supportive—many even got off the trail, or at least move to the other side—a few ruined it for the rest with some yelling at us for "using their trail." But aside from those bikers, the day was going well so far.

The fourth aid station went smooth as silk. The crew seemed to be finding its groove and I was in and out in no time at all. As I was leaving I told them to give my apologies to Rich for unceremoniously ditching him.

The last leg was approximately 4.1 miles of rocky hell. While the hills were about the same as the rest of the course, the trails were decidedly more technical. I would grow to hate this leg as the day wore on.

During the beginning of this first loop I was feeling good, perhaps due to the two pints of Ben and Jerry's® I consumed. I was ahead of my time predictions, but then, about half way, I suddenly started to crash. It was totally unexpected. My pace slowed, I didn't have any energy, and my motivation suddenly disappeared. This wasn't supposed to happen this early and I started to panic.

As the lap progressed, I went through my mental checklist of possible causes. I was going okay with hydration and electrolytes, and had plenty of calories. Maybe it was a sudden blood sugar crash due to all the calories from the coffee cake and ice cream. I decided I needed some protein.

I could snag something at the start/finish line, which was about a half mile away.

To help keep my feet dry, I spontaneously decided to take my Vibrams off for this section. It felt good to strip my damp socks and shoes off, and the dirt under my feet felt cool and refreshing. This new sensation provided a barely-perceivable boost to my worsening mood.

The trail leading to the start/finish line was fairly rough, but I was alert enough to easily avoid the small, sharp rocks. I traversed a few hills, hit the cut-grass path, turned the last corner, passed by a cheering crowd sitting around the fire pit, ran down a small hill, and crossed the line to finish my first lap.

Only five more to go.

The tent at the start/finish was a busy place with lots of runners and plenty of food. I ate a turkey sandwich and a cup of chicken noodle soup. However, I didn't see my crew. Perhaps they got caught up waiting for Rich. I exited the tent and started the quarter mile run to the trail head. As I crested the last grassy hill of the park, I saw my entire crew cheering loudly. They had set up a chair near the trail head. Their logic was simple—it was close to the RV. That worked out well allowing me to do my aid station routine without having to deal with the traffic at the aid station. I didn't tell my crew that I felt like garbage. Instead I just smiled, did my thing, and then hit the trail again.

Lap two started badly as it took awhile to get out of the funk, though eventually my mood did improve. Still suspecting the sugar buzz as the culprit, I was questioning the logic of the Ben and Jerry's shakes. When I got to the first aid station on lap two, I took one sip and gagged. I was officially past the point where I could tolerate sugary food and instead asked for the pancakes. I swapped my water bottle again, replaced my Succeed E-caps, changed shirts, and was about to re-lube. When I asked for it, Jason pulled it out of his pants. I'm pretty sure it wasn't in his pocket, rather actually down the front of his pants. That moment provided a perfect snapshot of my crew.

I re-lubed, grabbed some pancakes, and hit the trail. After about 100 yards, I tried eating one but as soon as I put it in my mouth, I gagged. Damn! Just like the ice cream shakes, the pancakes caused me to gag. I knew this was a serious problem because the only other food items I brought were hotdogs, and I didn't have enough to sustain me for the entire race. I don't remember a lot from this leg because I pretty much spent the entire three or four miles choking down quarter-sized pancake pieces.

Just before I got to the next aid station, I remembered I had packed some chia seeds in my gear—almost as an afterthought. I had experimented with them in training, but never thought of them as a primary fuel source. But, if it works for the Taramuhara, maybe it could work for me.

As soon as I got to the second aid station of the second loop, I asked Shelly to get the chia. I lubed up, replaced my packet of electrolytes, and checked my pace. Michael was doing an awesome job of recording my times. I was still on about a 22 hour pace. Perfect.

Shelly brought me the canister of chia seeds. I didn't think about the best method to eat them, so I just took a scoop and dumped it in my mouth. It felt a little like eating fine kitty litter. Almost immediately I gagged, then choked on the tiny seeds as they instantly absorbed the saliva from my mouth. I instinctively tried to swallow which  only caused me to cough and seeds sprayed everywhere. I'm pretty sure my crew, the aid station volunteers, and the other runners were laughing at that point. I then grabbed a cup of water, dumped another scoop of seeds in the cup, and pounded the seedy water mixture. It went down easily. Success!

At that point, one of the aid station volunteers started asking questions about the Vibrams. Though I tried to avoid being rude, I had to cut him off because I had spent WAY too much time at that aid station. I told my crew to have some chia ready at the next aid station and hit the trail, not knowing if I could keep eating the chia for the whole race, but it was worth a shot.

The next short leg was uneventful. My crew met me on the path just before the third aid station. There I went through my usual routine. I was handed a bottle of chia and water, but it looked like it had been mixed for thirty minutes or so. Since chia absorbs water, it had turned into a thick gel that was Jello-like. I turned the bottle upside down and the chia just stuck to the bottom of the bottle. Frantically I started dumping any liquid I could find into the bottle and shaking it up in an attempt to get the chia out. It worked, but was pretty disgusting and had little taste. The texture reminded me of frog eggs scooped from the mud of a pond.

I left this stop quickly since the actual aid station was only about a quarter mile down the trail. Since I was already supplied, I just grabbed a Gu, gave them my number, and took off. For a fleeting moment I felt like an elite runner.

The next section was fun. I met up with Brian Thomas whose lupusrunner.org blog I had read a few weeks earlier. He had recently finished Burning River (the race I did not finish the previous year). His 100-mile advice was deceptively simple: "Keep moving!" which actually served me well later in the race. We swapped positions throughout the day. I believe he later experienced ankle pain and wisely DNFed after the fourth lap.

I also met up with Dusty, a friend from the *Kickrunners* running forum. She had given me a lot of tips for running that particular trail as she trains there often. It was cool to finally meet her in person.

The lap was turning into a major social event. A few minutes after separating from Dusty, I met Scotchkee, another friend from the *Kickrunners* forum. He was running the 50-miler as a training run for the Javalina Jundred in a few weeks (which he later ran for his first 100-mile finish!). Together, these three made it an interesting and fast loop. Somewhere in there, I stopped at the fourth aid station of the loop for the usual treatment.

In that the last leg, I met up with Jesse Scott who is another barefoot runner, though he just started. He was running the

50K and was looking great. We talked for a minute, and then he was off. I would see him at the finish later—his first ultra was a success. Since the race, Jesse and I have shared many ideas on barefoot and minimalist shoe running. I believe he has a bright future in the world of ultramarathons.

I was getting excited. When I passed the start/finish, I'd get Shelly as my first pacer. Having her as a pacer was a major boost. I was feeling pretty good anyway, but that really added to the fun.

That lap would be a major challenge for Shelly. The farthest she had ever run was 15.5 miles, and that was two kids ago. Because our youngest son was five months old, her training was somewhat limited. To add to the challenge, she has only run trails a handful of times.

On loop two, I realized Shelly was behind the awesome organization of the crew at each aid station. Before taking her away to pace, I asked her to make a list of duties for the rest of the crew. I did not have tremendous confidence in the remainder of the crew's ability to stay organized.

The aid station stops throughout this loop went pretty smooth. It was the first point where my feet started looking as if they were being tortured. Though they felt fine, my feet were becoming a bit macerated from sweat with the skin turning white and looking as if it was going to fall off.

During this lap, I briefly ran with another guy running the 50-miler. We talked about my feet after he asked about the

Vibrams. I told him about the macerated skin and he reminded me about putting lube on your feet to essentially waterproof them. At the next aid station, I liberally coated my feet in SportSlick before I put on the Injinjis and Vibrams. That turned out to be a winning combination. Throughout the rest of the race, I developed only three dime-sized blisters and the macerated skin was limited to the damage already done.

As we neared the end of the lap, I was a bit sad. I would miss the opportunity to talk to Shelly except for the brief 30-second, "How are you feeling?" conversations at the aid stations. Still, she was looking a bit rough toward the end of the lap. The long miles and rough trails had taken their toll.

As we neared the finish line, I gave Shelly my water bottle to swap while I grabbed some food at the finish line tent. The food selection was improving as the shorter races had ended. I grabbed four pieces of pizza, a hunk of turkey sandwich, and a cup of beef broth as I walked to the waiting crew at the trail head. That pizza may be the best I've ever eaten—at least it sure seemed like it at the time.

The Halfway Point

Lap four was Mark's lap. We had run together a few times in training, so I was familiar with his pace. I knew I could count on him to keep me moving if I ran into trouble. In my previous  100, this is where I crashed and burned. This time I was feeling pretty good as the lap began. It was during this lap where the haziness set it. Even though I felt pretty good, the memories are a jumbled mess. The aid stations became indistinguishable and each hill felt like the rest.

The trails were now nearly empty. All the shorter races were done and most of the 50-milers had finished. Darkness would be setting in soon. I started having problems with hand chafing early in the lap, so I begin using one of my most embarrassing pieces of equipment, a pair of women's stretch-knit gloves. Luckily I had packed my black pair and not the hot pink ones. That kept the ridicule in check.

I was still pretty warm, so I only wore one on my water bottle hand. Someone on the crew commented it was a tribute to Michael Jackson, who had recently died. Now, if only I could moonwalk ...

Darkness fell sometime around the middle of the lap. I really don't remember exactly when. We picked up our lights at the second aid station. I was using a Fenix handheld which has served me well. Most night runners prefer a headlamp, but I find the handheld provides better terrain recognition.

At some point, I was worried about being cold so I asked my crew to get my pants. I think they were surprised by my cotton pajama pants, plaid pattern and all. They went well with my Gap sweatshirt. After taking flak about my attire, I decided to temporarily forgo the pants. I would run in shorts the rest of the way.

That lap also saw the onset of my first knee pain when running down hills. I have a chronic patellar tendon injury from pitching baseballs and the injury sometimes flares up when running downhill for hours. While it severely slowed my downhill pace, it was manageable.

The mid-point aid station was absolutely fabulous at night and the volunteers were awesome. They gave me some sweet tea which provided an immediate boost. I also appreciated their support and reassurances that I looked great.

On the last leg of that lap, I stubbed my pinky toe on my right foot for the first time. It felt as if I had ripped it off, but it didn't affect my gait and I was able to continue without breaking stride. I also felt the beginnings of a hotspot on the bottom of both heels where blisters would eventually form. This wasn't a huge issue, but it had been a long time since I ran with a blister.

At some point, Mark asked if I would do this again. As much as I wanted to say "No!", I knew this wouldn't be the last time. As would be the pattern for the last three laps, the last leg became a hellish walk-fest. Thankfully, the people at the finish line at this point were VERY supportive and it was great to experience. If not for the support of my crew, I may have considered quitting at this point. The true value of a crew and pacers becomes apparent at this juncture in a race.

Lap five was Michael's lap. He would be with me from eleven p.m. Saturday night until around five a.m. Sunday morning. Based on our email exchanges, I knew he would keep me moving at all costs. He was also our time management expert throughout the race. Even in my diminished state, I knew I would finish if I could keep moving.

We had what I vaguely remember as great conversations but I cannot remember exactly what we talked about. I think we discussed food, real estate, and a lot of running. Most of what we discussed is just a distant blur.

I felt pretty good this whole lap, but I walked almost the entire time. The pain was getting pretty bad, though I felt strong mentally. There were no signs of the complete crash I experienced at Burning River. I remember Mark taking pictures at each aid station and hallucinating about weird things in the depths of the forest. I saw a lot of buildings, out-houses mostly. I'm sure Sigmund Freud would have something to say about that.

At the end of the lap I had discussed the possibility of taking a 15 minute nap to reset my circadian cycles and ward off involuntary sleep. But I wasn't feeling tired as the loop ended, so I didn't mention it. I found out later that the crew wouldn't have let me, even though I still think I could have handled it if I'd had a bigger time cushion. Oddly, I don't remember going through the finish line tent at all. However, I DO remember seeing Stuart.

As I walked over the last hill before the trail head, my light illuminated what appeared to be a giant burning flare. As I got closer, I realized it was Stuart wearing an incredibly reflective crossing guard-style shirt. It was blindingly bright. I would have no problem finding him in the darkness.

We set off on the final loop. I knew my time would be fairly close, so I dug deep and managed to run some flats with Stuart. Almost immediately, he started telling stories though I forgot 90% of them. I do remember being thoroughly entertained by Stuart talking about his memoirs, "My Life as a Dork." His stories about growing up as a dork had a profoundly positive impact on the person he is today and I could relate to every one of them. It was a strangely powerful moment. Then I snapped back to reality remembering I had run about 88 miles so far.

Stuart was really pushing the pace. I didn't want to run, but had to in order to keep up with him. My quads finally started to get fatigued to the point where the hills felt difficult. The problem was compounded by a feeling of sleepiness that was hitting me in ever-strengthening waves.

As if he could sense my struggles, Stuart broke into show tunes. I don't remember what songs were sung, but I do remember Stuart's hauntingly beautiful voice. It felt as if I were dreaming. Granted, it was a dream filled with sharp dagger-like pains from blisters, a strange grinding pain in my knees, a searing pain in the back of my right knee and quads, and a myriad of other seemingly traveling pains caused by a combination of fatigue, overuse, and friction. The pain was beginning to fade as I began to relax. Stuart's singing was fading slowly and the dream abruptly ended when I felt myself falling. Somehow I managed to catch myself before hitting the ground and it took a few seconds to realize I was running. It was dark. I could still hear Stuart singing, his bright crossing guard shirt easily visible in the beam of my light. Unbelievably, I had just fallen asleep while running on a flat boardwalk. Damn that was scary!

I continued to trudge on wishing the sun would come up. I think we passed a few runners during this stage, and some may have passed us, too. My memories are VERY fuzzy.

Somewhere between the first and second aid station, the sun came up. Experienced 100-milers say it makes a huge difference, and it does. The sun coming up was an immediate boost and the sleepy grogginess faded. I felt alert.

Unfortunately daylight brought more mountain bikers. When the first group passed us the lead biker shouted out, "Four of us!" as he whizzed past. A few seconds later another passed, followed a few minutes later by the third. The fourth bike never came by, which seemed odd. Then about 20 minutes later, the lead biker came back and asked us if we had seen his friend, the fourth rider. We hadn't, so he continued to backtrack.

About a half hour later, we saw him again. Stuart asked if he found him yet to which the guy replied, "No, I'm checking all the other trails." Perhaps channeling some of my new-found disdain for mountain bikers, Stuart quipped, "Don't worry; I'm checking all the ditches!" I laughed a little, realized it hurt too much, and continued shuffling along.

Eventually we started to meet a few recreational runners running in the opposite direction. Most had been on the trail Saturday morning. It was surreal to think I'd been running for over 24 hours at that point.

When we pulled into the last aid station, I knew it was almost over. By this time I was getting very tired of running and just wanted it to end. It was a lot like getting a tattoo. The constant pain, while tolerable in the short-term, begins to play games with your mind. I now understand how people DNF at mile 95 of a 100-mile race. The previous 95 miles were inconsequential. All I could see was the four-plus mile mountain of the race that remained.

My entire crew was going to hike the rest of the course with me to the finish. I was glad they would be there to keep me company, especially Shelly. Her feet had taken a horrific beating on the lap she paced with me. She described the feeling as "if my toenails came off in my socks." Needless to say, she couldn't fit her swollen, painful feet into her shoes, so she put three or four pairs of socks on her feet. It looked as if she were wearing giant puffy pillows. I think the crew made a joke of it, but I wasn't coherent enough to understand.

We started hiking this long, hellish, rock-filled leg. It started pretty well. Though I was tired and in a lot of pain, I was still pretty much "there" mentally. At some point, I stopped to relieve myself on the side of the trail. I noticed a tree immediately to my left had what appeared to be a mouth and it was chewing something while making a corresponding chewing noise. Then it winked at me. Okay, maybe I wasn't as mentally sound as I thought.

My last solid memory of that last leg was of Michael exclaiming, "My ass-crack hurts!" which brought an immediate reply about Jason spooning the rest of the crew as they napped and the tube of lube he kept in his pants. I remember laughing. Then nothing.

The remainder of that leg was a strange memory of looking into a tunnel and hearing muffled voices around me. I hallucinated something about a flower picking incident, and of a bee flying around me. Additionally I remember feeling very emotional with the realization that I was finally going to fulfill my long-standing goal, but it felt dream-like.

The Finish

Eventually we made it to the asphalt, the landmark that indicated about three quarters of a mile left. I remember that clearly because it made me realize that the end was near, which caused me to snap out of my trance-like condition.

With Shelly by my side, I walked the small asphalt hill, turned right on the trail, traversed a few hills, and hit the mowed grass of the park. There were a few people milling about who started clapping and yelling encouragements. I crossed the field, turned down a small hill, then turned toward the finish line. With fifty yards left, I managed to break into a pathetic run.

Running under that finish line sign was one of the greatest feelings I have ever experienced. It was both the realization of a long-held dream and the knowledge that I could finally stop running. The sense of accomplishment wouldn't hit me until the following Monday.

Twenty-nine hours and five minutes after starting, I had finished running 100 miles. I shook the hand of the race director as he placed a medal over my head and handed me my buckle. It was an amazing feeling. I then shook the hands of my crew, thanking each one for helping me reach this pinnacle and then, finally, hugged Shelly. I had been fighting back my emotions for the entire leg and holding her in my arms at that very moment was one of the best moments of my life. That hug was the culmination of the transformation I had begun many months earlier. Those rock-laden rolling hills through the rural trails of Pinckney had served as a metaphor for my life. Now I stood at the end, victorious in the arms of the woman I love. There will be other 100-milers, but this one will always be special.

Hallucination 100 buckle and the Vibrams used in the race

Appendix

Barefoot and Minimalist Shoe Runners and Supporters You Should Know

Ken Bob Saxton:
Widely considered to be the leader of the barefoot running movement. His website (http://thebarefootrunning.com) is considered "must-read" material. Most of my theories were developed from Ken Bob's teachings. He is the "resident guru" of the Barefoot Runners Society.

"Barefoot" Rick Roeber:
Best known for his string of barefoot marathons. Rick's ideas, disseminated through his website (http://barefootrunner. org), were a major influence on my early barefoot running experiences.

Ted McDonald:
Barefoot Ted's most famous appearance came in Christopher McDougall's excellent book *Born to Run*. Before that appearance, Ted shared a great deal of experience through his website (http://barefootted.com). Ted was the other major influence on my early barefoot running adventures.

Abebe Bikila:
Bikila won the 1960 Olympic Marathon while running barefoot. The Olympic games that year were sponsored by Adidas but the shoes Bikila was given were ill-fitting. Since he trained barefoot, he made the decision to run the race without shoes.

Angela Bishop:
Writer of the popular *Barefoot Angie Bee* blog (http:// barefoot-angieb.blogspot.com). She routinely writes about her experiences as a barefoot runner and mother while providing a ton of tremendous product reviews.

Zola Budd (Pieterse):
Budd is a South African woman that held the 5000 meter world record in the 1980s. At her peak, she trained and competed barefoot.

Mark Cucuzzella, MD:
Cucuzzella is a physician, ultrarunner, race director, and owner of Two Rivers Treads (http://www.trtreads.org), a minimalist running store in West Virginia. Mark also spends considerable time educating runners about proper running form.

Preston Curtis:
Long-time barefoot runner from the Boston, Massachusetts area, Preston's Metro Boston Barefoot Runners group (www.meetup.com/Metro-Boston-Barefoot-Runners) has been instrumental at promoting and supporting barefoot running. He is also one of the charter members of the Barefoot Runners Society.

Irene Davis, PhD, PT, FACSM:
Professor of physical therapy at the University of Delaware. Davis' research is investigating the relationships between lower extremities, mechanics, and injury.

Tina DuBois:
Tina runs the Living Barefoot website (http://www.livingbarefoot.info) which exists to promote a barefoot lifestyle, including walking, running, and products associated with the barefoot lifestyle. She is also a co-host of the *Living Barefoot* podcast and writes the *Toe Girl Tina's Barefoot Alternative Adventures* blog.

Herb Elliott:
Winner of the gold medal in the 1500 meters at the 1960 Olympic Games who also ran 17 sub-four minute miles. He was never defeated in a 1500 meter or mile race.

Joseph Froncioni, MD:
Orthopedic surgeon and runner, Froncioni wrote one of the most influential works of the modern barefoot running movement mentioned earlier in this book. The essay can also be found on his blog (http://www.quickswood.com/my_weblog/2006/08/athletic_footwe.html).

Al Gauthier:
Runs the Living Barefoot website (http://www.livingbarefoot.info) which exists to promote a barefoot lifestyle and includes walking, running, and products associated with the barefoot lifestyle. Al is also a co-host of the *Living Barefoot* podcast.

Tamara Gerken:
Creator of the *Runners World* Barefoot Running Forum, which is a valuable meeting place to share ideas about barefoot running. Tamara is also a founding member and first president of the Barefoot Runners Society, the leading organization on all things related to barefoot running.

Cameron Guthrie:
One of the founding members of the Barefoot Runners Society, Cameron is the original designer and webmaster of the BRS site, and is responsible for many of the design aspects of the organization.

Scott Hadley, PhD, DPT:
Hadley is a pioneer in developing treatment procedures for all runners in general, and barefoot runners in particular. He is also a leader in the study of reflexes and running gait.

Daniel Howell, PhD:
Associate professor of biology at Liberty University, Howell is also the author of *The Barefoot Book*. (http://www.drdanielhowell.com)

Anton Krupica:
Minimalist shoe elite ultramarathon runner known for his very high mileage training and wins in the Miwok, Leadville, and Rocky Raccoon 100-mile races.

Erwan LeCorre:
Founder of the Natural Movement Coaching System® as featured on his MoveNat website (http://movnat.com.)

Jessica Lee:
Founder and president of runBARE (http://runbare.com), a barefoot running school in Boulder, Colorado. Jessica is also a contributor to the book *Barefoot Running: How to Run Light and Free by Getting in Touch with the Earth*.

Daniel Lieberman, PhD:
Professor of human evolutionary biology at Harvard University, he has conducted research on the impact forces of barefoot versus shod running. Lieberman's ongoing research is testing the merits of barefoot versus shod running. His excellent Web contributions can be found at (http://www.barefootrunning.fas.harvard.edu).

Christopher McDougall:
Journalist and author of *Born to Run*, which has energized and publicized the barefoot running movement. Since its publication, McDougall has become an outspoken critic of the modern running shoe.

Justin Owings:
Owner of Birthday Shoes (http://birthdayshoes.com) his site is dedicated to minimalist shoes in general and Vibram's Five Fingers in particular.

Victor Palma:
Long-time barefoot runner who helped found the Barefoot Runners Society. Victor has been a tireless supporter of the barefoot running movement, including advocating barefoot running in the military.

Jesse Scott:
Scott is an accomplished minimalist shoe runner from Muskegon, Michigan. Jesse has at least one ultramarathon win and was involved in a photo-finish at the North Country Trail 50 miler in Manistee, Michigan in 2010. Jesse is also one of the founding members of the "Hobby Joggas" running club and prolific blogger. His blog can be found at http://jscott87. blogspot.com.

Todd Ragsdale:
Barefoot ultramarathon runner who in June of 2010, broke the Guinness World Record for farthest distance covered in 24 hours while barefoot.

Steven Robbins, MD:
Prominent researcher on barefoot running. Steven began publishing his barefoot research in 1987. His website (http://www.stevenrobbinsmd.com/home) contains the full text of his research.

Julian Romero:
The elder barefoot Romero brother has dominated marathons by routinely posting sub-three hour times repeatedly. Julian also placed second in the Duke City Marathon.

Alex Romero:
The younger barefoot Romero brother also has multiple sub-three hour marathons to his credit, including a win in the Duke City Marathon.

Leif Rustvold:
Barefoot and minimalist shoe ultramarathon runner, Leif has run a 100-mile race in Vibram Five Fingers. His "Distance Minimally" blog documents his adventures (http://www.distanceminimally.com)

Michael Sandler:
Author of the excellent barefoot running book *Barefoot Running: How to Run Light and Free by Getting in Touch with the Earth.* Michael is also a barefoot running educator and founder of runBARE (http://runbare.com), a barefoot running school in Boulder, Colorado.

Shivnath Singh:
Considered India's greatest distance runner, Singh was also known for competing with only tape on his feet. In international competition, he won a gold medal and five silvers.

Shelly Robillard:
Shelly is a long-distance barefoot and minimalist shoe runner and my lovely wife! Shelly is known for her the work she does to inspire others to meet their greatest goals. Shelly's blog can be found at http://shoelessshelbell.blogspot.com.

Jason Spooner:
Barefoot runner best known for his high mileage training, Spooner routinely runs more than 100 miles per week barefoot, including a 155+ mile week. He has also run a sub-three hour barefoot marathon.

Patrick Sweeney:
Barefoot/minimalist runner from Manhattan Beach, California. Sweeney won the Palos Verdes Marathon in 2010 while wearing Vibram Five Fingers. He is also an accomplished ultramarathon runner.

James Webber:
Barefoot runner from Kalamazoo, Michigan, James routinely places at or near the top of every race he runs, making him one of the fastest barefoot runners in the United States. His accomplishments include a 2:46 marathon.

Finding Other Barefoot and Minimalist Shoe Runners

Until a few years ago, most barefoot runners lived a lonely existence. While there were a handful of "barefoot hotspots," most of us toiled in obscurity. For myself, I ran barefoot for four years before I had the opportunity to run with another barefoot runner.

The rise in popularity of barefoot running has led to two major changes. Since there are more barefoot runners, there is a great likelihood you will encounter others. Also, many barefoot runners maintain a presence on the Internet, which can be a wonderful resource to learn from. The Internet also provides an opportunity to meet people in your area.

In the fall of 2009, several barefoot runners, myself included, decided to help facilitate the meeting process by forming the Barefoot Runners Society (http://barefootrunners.org). The organization is a non-profit organization with chapters around the country. Odds are good that a chapter exists in your area. If not, contact the BRS leadership and inquire about starting a local chapter.

The Barefoot Runners Society

The Barefoot Runners Society was born out of a strong desire to connect with others who share the same passion for running barefoot that I do. This connection is what binds us to one another and helps us to feel that we are not alone in this otherwise solitary experience. Forum discussions were nice, but I felt I needed more. Why just talk about running barefoot together? Why not run barefoot together? I knew that if I had this need, then surely others did too. It must have been fate because I managed to find a web designer, Cameron Guthrie, who was also a barefoot runner, who lived in my state, and who had the same vision I did. We hit the jackpot again when Jason Robillard, Victor Palma, Preston Curtis, and Haley DiCicco agreed to join on. I couldn't ask for a better group to work with. In order to foster this sense of community, we decided early on to share and delegate some of the responsibility for this project to very capable barefoot and minimalist runners interested in helping us to grow the vision and ideals of the BRS. We have recruited volunteers to work for the BRS in all capacities from legal counsel, to a CPA, to writers, to photographers, to marketing reps, etc. If you are a barefoot or minimalist runner, be sure to join the Barefoot Runners Society to take advantage of the many resources we have to offer at no charge to you at www.barefootrunners.org. With their help and possibly yours, we will grow our crazy sport, and per Jason, "Change the running world one odd look at a time."

Tamara Gerken,
Barefoot Runners Society president and founding member

Barefoot Running Testimonials

The following stories come from members of the *Runner's World* Barefoot Forum. Each has a different story to share about how barefoot running can be a wonderfully rewarding experience.

"For me, barefoot running re-introduced a childhood-like joy that had been missing most of my life. There is little to compare with the feeling of the ground beneath your bare feet as you are quietly and softly running along. I feel more connected with nature and myself. And I've saved countless hundreds of dollars over the last decade on unnecessary shoes and socks! So, for me, I run barefoot for the pure joy and fun of it. I can't even imagine running any other way anymore."

—Victor Palma

"I have Morton's Neuroma, a pre-running condition. It really started to bother me when I increased my mileage. One day I was out running a 10K distance with my hubby who was pushing our boys in a double jogger when around mile 5, I began to feel a horrible searing, burning pain under the toes on my left foot. I was in so much pain, I thought I had fractured my toes. I stopped, sat down, took my shoes off, and started rubbing my toes. The pain went away immediately. I thought that was odd, so I decided to leave my shoes off and catch up to them. I finished that run feeling as though I was onto something. I found that running barefoot allows me to run much farther than I could shod. Looking back now, I think that run was by far the best run I have ever had, not in terms of quality but awareness of how important running is to me. I thank God for Morton's Neuroma, for without it, I would never have discovered running barefoot.

—Tamara Gerken

"Six months ago, I started running barefoot on hard surfaces. Prior to that, I ran for three years with running shoes. I started to get very bad pains in my knee, even when walking. I was starting to limp and couldn't walk up the stairs. I tried those worthless knee straps which didn't work. I went to a Sports Medicine Doctor. He indicated that because of relatively weak thigh muscles and a lack of proper foot support, my knees were becoming inflamed. (Odd, I have no support barefoot and the pain is gone.) He told me to relieve the pain by icing my knees immediately after running and to take an anti-inflammatory like ibuprofen or aspirin after running. The doctors like to treat the symptoms but not address the problem.

One day, I did a search on Google®. I typed in 'knee hurts while running' and found barefoot running sites, did the research, and it made sense. I started barefoot running, and the knee pain went away within one week. I haven't had any knee pain for six months now. I look forward to running now. I never have to ice any joints, and I don't have to take aspirin. This weekend I ran a 5K. A woman asked me if it hurts to run barefoot. I told her, "No. I started running barefoot to take away knee pain." She replied that she doesn't get knee pain either with shoes because she gets cortisone shots in the knee! I feel this is treating the symptom and not the problem. Barefoot running saves money!!! No running shoes, no sports medicine doctor fees or medicine!
—Barefoot Larry

"I was "born to wear orthotics and knee braces." I used barefoot running to recover from a semi-serious injury, and I've gotten faster after adapting a midfoot strike with minimal footwear. Before running, I was an overweight asthma patient with Osgood-Schlatter's syndrome. I was told orthotics and heavy cushioning, along with knee braces, were essential to my health. I thought I would feel pain for the rest of my life and running just wasn't for me. I would never be one of those 'naturally gifted' runners.

I started running barefoot to improve my form, but it didn't take long for me to start thinking about ditching traditional running shoes altogether. Once I became familiar with myself and my form, my runs were no longer limited to the amount of pain I could withstand. Taking off big, clunky shoes has allowed my feet to teach me about my body and feel the signals that teach me how to run.

My season has consisted of running several races and competing in several triathlons and has been a season of transition. I completed my first half-Ironman triathlon and an off-road 50K race. The longer races were with shoes, but I have full confidence that I

will be ready to repeat these performances, as well as a 50-mile ultra, either barefoot or in minimalist footwear.

Running barefoot, in my experience, has been completely absent of the typical symptoms involved with shod running. My leg muscles have not been sore, I have had no joint swelling, and my recovery has been overnight in the longest of cases."

—Jesse Scott

Barefoot Resources

- Barefoot Running UniversityTM (http://barefootrunninguniversity.com)—My barefoot and ultramarathon site
- Shelly's Blog (http://shoelessshelbell.blogspot.com/) Shelly shares her journey through life, including stories about parenting, running, and her journey toward self-improvement.
- Robillard Adventures (http://robillardadventures.com/) The documentation of my family's adventures, including our long-term travel around the United States in an RV.

- Barefoot Runners Society (http://barefootrunners.org)
- Ken Bob Saxton's website (http://therunningbarefoot.com/)
- *Runner's World*® barefoot running forum (http://www. runnersworld. com/community/forums/index.jsp)
- Birthday Shoes (http://birthdayshoes.com)
- Borntorun.org (http://borntorun.org)
- Barefoot Rick Roeber's website (http://www.barefootrunner.org/)
- runBARE (http://runbare.com)
- Yahoo® Group for Barefoot Runners (http://sports.groups.yahoo.com/group/RunningBarefoot)
- Barefoot Ted's Google Group for huaraches (http://groups.google.com/group/huaraches)—Mexican sandals used for running
- Barefoot Ted's website (http://www.barefootted.com/)
- Evolution Running® (http://www.evolutionrunning.com)
- Good Form Running® (http://www.goodformrunning.com/)
- POSE® method of running—article about barefoot running (http://posetech.com/)
- Wikipedia article about barefoot running (http://en.wikipedia.org/wiki/Barefoot_running)
- Chi Running® Method (http://www.chirunning.com/shop/home.php)
- Crossfit Grand Rapids® (http://crossfitgr.com/)
- Crossfit® (http://crossfit.com)
- Crossfit Endurance® (http://crossfitendurance.com)

Glossary

Barefoot Running (BFR)—Running with nothing on your feet.

Cadence—How many times each foot touches the ground, usually measured per minute. Barefoot cadence is usually greater than shod cadence with most barefoot coaches recommending a cadence of at least 180.

Fartlek Run—Run with varying levels of intensity ranging from walking to sprinting.

Hill Work—Running up and down hills. Done either as a continuous run or as repeats.

Long Run—A continuous run over a long distance at a slow speed used to build endurance.

Minimalist Running (MR)—Running in shoes that provide limited or no support and only minimal protection. Also, the heel will be at the same level as the forefoot. Examples include Vibram FiveFingers®, Feelmax® shoes, aqua socks (or beach shoes), or some racing flats. MR is often an acceptable second choice to BFR from an injury-prevention standpoint.

Over-Striding—The tendency for a runner's foot to make contact in front of their center of gravity resulting in a "braking" action. Common among heel-strikers. Leads to decreased running efficiency and may be a major cause of running injuries.

Reduced Shoe Running (RSR)—Running in a shoe that provides less support and less cushioning than a traditional running shoe but still causes many of the same problems as traditional running shoes. The heel of RSRs will be slightly higher than the forefoot area. Nike Frees and most racing flats are examples of RSR.

Speed Work—Fast-paced running above normal running pace. Usually involves running repeats over a given distance (run fast for a short time, recover, then repeat).

Stride Length—Distance between successive points where one foot touches the ground. Barefoot stride length is typically shorter than shod stride length.

Tempo Run—Fast-paced run of intermediate length; runner speeds up as the run progresses until 10K pace is reached.

Too Much Too Soon (TMTS)—The tendency of new barefoot runners to run farther or faster than their body is capable of. Often results in injuries.

Top of Foot Pain (TOFP)—Pain experienced along the top of the foot. Strong top of the foot pain usually indicates the new barefoot runner is doing too much too soon. Some degree of mild, dull soreness is common as feet adapt to barefoot or minimalist running.

References

Baer, E. (1982). Babies mean business. *New Internationalist*, 110.

Bean, A. (1997). Expert Advice. *Runner's World*; 100–101.

Bemson, R. (1997). Trainerspotting. *Electronic Telegraph*, 6th December.

Bramble, D.M. & Lieberman, D.E. (2004). Endurance running and the evolution of homo. *Nature*, 432. 345–352.

Brunet, M.E., Cook, S.D., Brinker, M.R., Dickinson, J.A. (1990). A survey of running injuries in 1505 competitive and recreational runners. *Journal of Sports Medicine and Physical Fitness*, Vol 30, No 3, 307–315.

Clement, D.B., Taunton, J.E., Smart, G.W., McNicol, K.L. (1981). A Survey of Overuse Running Injuries. *The Physician and Sports Medicine*, Vol 9, No 5, 47–58.

Craig R., Parker J., & Callister R. (2008). *British Journal of Sports Medicine*. Published Online First: 18 April 2008.Cudicio, R., "L'étude Qui Fait Peur Aux Géants". Sport et Vie, Jan Feb 1998, No 46.

D'Assche, G. (1997). History of the trainer. *Electronic Telegraph*, 6th December.

Eccles J.C., Fatt P., Landgren, S. (1956). Central pathway for direct inhibitory action of impulses in largest afferent nerve fibres to muscle. *Journal of Neurophysiology*, 19(1):75–98.

Froncioni, J. (2006). Athletic footwear and running injuries. Article posted to http://www.quickswood.com/my_weblog/2006/08/athletic_footwe.html.

Gregoriada, X. (1998). Will this one run and run? *The Independent on Sunday*, 1st February.

Gwyther, M. (1997). Smelly old trainers, £300. *Electronic Telegraph*, 15th February.

Hamill, J. & Bates, B.T. (1988). A kinetic evaluation of the effects of in vito loading on running shoes. *Journal of Orthopaedic and Sports Physical Therapy*, 10(2): 47–53.

Kleinke, C.L., Peterson, T.R., Rutledge, T.R. (1998). Effects of self-generated facial expressions on mood. *Journal of Personality and Social Psychology*, 74(1): 272–279.

Lebow, F., Averbuen, G., and Friends. (1994). The New York Road Runners Club Complete Book of Running (Updated Edition). *New York Road Runners Club*.

Lieberman, D.E., et. al. (2010). Foot strike patterns and collision forces in habitually barefoot versus shod runners. *Nature*, 463: 531–536.

Marti, B. (1998). Relationships between running injuries and running shoes—results of a study of 5,000 participants of a 16K run. *The Shoe in Sport*. Chicago: Year Book Medical Publishers. 256–265.

McNitt-Gray, J.L., Takashi, Y., Millward, C. (1993). Landing Strategy Adjustments Made by Female Gymnasts in Response to Drop Height and Mat Composition. *Journal of Applied Biomechanics*, 9, 173–190.

Rao, U.B., Joseph, B. (1992). The Influence of Footwear on the Prevalence of Flat Foot, a Survey of 2300 Children. *The Journal of Bone and Joint Surgery*, July Vol 74-B; No. 4, 525–527.

Robbins, S.E., Gouw, G.J. (1990). "Athletic Footwear and Chronic Overloading A Brief Review. *Sports Medicine*, 9 (2): 76–85.

Robbins, S.E., Gouw, G.J. (1991). Athletic footwear: unsafe due to perceptual illusions. *Medicine and Science in Sports and Exercise*, Vol 23, No2, 217–224.

Robbins, S.E., Gouw, G.J., Hanna, A.M. (1989). Running-related injury prevention through innate impact-moderating behaviour. *Medicine and Science in Sports and Exercise*. Vol 21, No2, 130–139.

Robbins, S., Gouw, G.J., McClaran, J., Waked, E. (1993). Protective Sensation of the Plantar Aspect of the Foot. *Foot & Ankle*, July/August Vol 14, No 6, 347–352.

Robbins, S., Hanna, A.M. (1987). Running-related injury prevention through barefoot adaptations. *Medicine and Science in Sports and Exercise*. Vol 19, No 2, 148–156.

Robbins, S.E., Hanna, A.M., Gouw, G.J. (1988). Overload protection: avoidance response to heavy plantar surface loading. *Medicine and Science in Sports and Exercise*. Vol 20, No 1, 85–92.

Robbins, Hanna, A., Jones, L.A. (1988). Sensory Attenuation Induced by Modern Athletic Footwear. *Journal of Testing and Evaluation.* Vol 16, 412–416.

Robbins, S., Waked, E. (1997). Balance and Vertical Impact in Sports: Role of Shoe Sole Materials. *Arch Phys Med Rehabil,* Vol 78, 463–467.

Robbins, S., Waked, E. (1998). Factors Associated with Ankle Injuries Preventative Measures. *Sports Medicine;* 25 (1): 63–72.

Robbins, S., Waked, E. (1997). Foot Position Awareness: The Effect of Footwear on Instability, Excessive Impact, and Ankle Spraining. *Critical Reviews in Physical and Rehabilitation Medicine,* 9 (1): 53–74.

Robbins, S., Waked, E. (1997). Hazard of deceptive advertising of athletic footwear. *British Journal of Sports Medicine;* 31:299–303.

Robbins, S., Waked, E., Gouw, G.J. McClaran, J. (1994). Athletic footwear affects balance in men. *British Journal of Sports Medicine;* 28(2) 117–123.

Sherrington, C.S. (1898). Experiments in examination of the peripheral distribution of the fibres of the posterior roots of some spinal nerves. *Philos. Trans. R. Soc. London Biol.* 190B:45–186.

Shulman, S.B (1949). Survey in China and India of feet that have never worn shoes. *The Journal of the National Association of Chiropodists,* 49, 26–30.

Stewart, S.F. (1972). Footgear—Its History, Uses and Abuses. *Clinical Orthopaedics and Related Research,* 88, 119–130.

Warburton, M. (2002). Barefoot Running, *Sportscience* 5(3), http://www.sportsci.org/jour/0103/mw.htm